"Writing from personal experience, Rick Johnson unequivocally understands the importance of a godly father in a girl's life. He gently navigates his readers through the tumultuous years of female puberty, the role of father as protector, and how to be the spiritual mentor every daughter needs. With lots of humor and personal stories, this book makes the frightening roller coaster ride of parenting a teen girl and transforms it into something practical and motivating. A must-read for every dad who desires a close relationship with his daughter!"

—Susie Shellenberger, editor, *SUSIE Magazine* for teen girls

"It's tough to be a girl in today's world. When a father picks up this book (or his sweet wife buys it for him), he will make an investment in his daughter's life. I am a firm believer that the father/daughter relationship is perhaps one of the most critical relationships in a young lady's life. If this book were on every father's nightstand, I daresay it wouldn't be as tough to be a girl in today's world."

—Vicki Courtney, author, 5 *Conversations You Must Have with Your Daughter*

"It takes diligent and timely seed planting to help your daughter blossom to be the woman that God meant her to be. With compassion and honesty, ideas and heart, Rick Johnson gives the tools needed for the growth of strength and godly beauty any parent wants for their daughter."

—Doug Fields, pastor, speaker, and author of *Fresh Start*

Other books by Rick Johnson

That's My Son
Better Dads, Stronger Sons
How to Talk So Your Husband Will Listen
The Power of a Man
Becoming Your Spouse's Better Half
That's My Teenage Son

Becoming the Dad *your* Daughter Needs

RICK JOHNSON

Revell

a division of Baker Publishing Group
Grand Rapids, Michigan

© 2012 by Rick Johnson

Published by Revell
a division of Baker Publishing Group
P.O. Box 6287, Grand Rapids, MI 49516-6287
www.revellbooks.com

ISBN 978-0-8007-2335-4

Printed in the United States of America

Previously published under the title *That's My Girl*

The Library of Congress has cataloged the previous edition as follows:
Johnson, Rick, 1956–
    That's my girl : how a father's love protects and empowers his daughter / Rick Johnson.
      p. cm.
    Includes bibliographical references (p.   ).
    ISBN 978-0-8007-3383-4 (pbk.)
    1. Fathers and daughters—Religious aspects—Christianity. 2. Child rearing—Religious aspects—Christianity. 3. Daughters—Religious life. I. Title.
    BV4529.17.J645 2012
    248.8'421—dc23
                                            2011030661

Published in association with the literary agency of WordServe Literary Group, Ltd., 10152 S. Knoll Circle, Highlands Ranch, CO 80130

The internet addresses, email addresses, and phone numbers in this book are accurate at the time of publication. They are provided as a resource. Baker Publishing Group does not endorse them or vouch for their content or permanence.

14 15 16 17 18 19 20   7 6 5 4 3 2 1

To Kelsey—my sweet baby girl.
And my "favorite" daughter.

Thanks, Hook.
May God heal
all the little "Hooks"
of the world.

Contents

Introduction

Fathers have incredible influence (positive or negative) on nearly every aspect of their daughter's life. A father sets a huge role model for his daughter regarding the qualities she looks for in a man and the standards she maintains in her relationships. He is the first man in her life and models how a man should treat a woman, how a man should act, and how a man shows healthy love and affection to a woman. He also sets the standard for how a daughter feels she deserves to be treated by men. He even determines how a girl feels about herself. If a father shows his daughter love, respect, and appreciation for who she is, she will believe that about herself as a woman, no matter what anyone else thinks. Girls deprived of this father love and affection make poor choices in an effort to fill that void.

One of the challenges about writing parenting books, at least for me, is I never really feel adequate to the task. Not having sterling role models while growing up, I never felt all that competent as a father or a parent. But both our children are young adults now, for the most part living on their own. While they have not chosen to necessarily be the people I envisioned them to be, I have to confess that they turned out to be pretty good people. They both have good morals, a good work ethic, and a strong value system (albeit slightly different from their parents').

Consequently, I did not enter into writing this book lightly. I admit, despite numerous requests from readers of my other books, I have been a bit reluctant and even apprehensive about writing a book for dads and daughters. My publisher suggested I write one several years ago, but I declined because frankly I didn't know if I was up to the task—especially while I was in the midst of raising a "slightly" rebellious teenage daughter. I guess I wanted to see how she turned out before I passed myself off as some sort of expert on the subject. Now, after guiding a very strong-willed daughter through the dangerous wilderness of adolescence into young adulthood, I feel a bit more competent to proceed. Understand, however, that raising daughters is as complicated as they are. Probably like most of you fathers out there, having been a boy and a son, I felt much more comfortable raising sons than I did daughters.

Frankly, boys have a much easier lot in life than girls. Girls are biologically much more complicated than boys. Indeed, females are more psychologically and physiologically complicated than their male counterparts as well. Females are much more holistic in the way they see and process the world around them. And females tend to be more emotionally driven than males, causing a plethora of challenges that males generally do not face.

In many ways I think raising daughters is much more complicated and difficult than raising sons. Certainly there are exceptions, but generally most people I speak to believe that girls present greater challenges than boys, possibly because the stakes are higher (or at least seem to be). Females appear to suffer most from poor decisions that are made by either sex. Women and girls suffer the consequences of poor decision making in nearly every circumstance. For instance, the vast majority of single parents are females, often raising their children without any support from the male sperm donor. Clearly a male was involved in the actions that contributed to producing a child, yet he does not suffer the consequences of his choices to nearly the degree that the female does.

What is it about a father-daughter relationship that is so powerful yet so frightening to a man? The entire time my daughter was growing up, I loved her like crazy—still do. I would have gladly thrown myself in front of a raging grizzly bear for her. But she scared the living daylights out of me, especially after she became a teenager. Her potential for self-destruction was in direct proportion to her inability to control herself. During adolescence she seemed unable or at least unwilling to view life from any kind of logical perspective. Her actions and decisions rarely made sense to me and often frustrated me beyond endurance. (Note: Throughout this book I share candidly about the ups and downs of our relationship. I do so with her full permission and knowledge.)

After numerous challenges over the years, my daughter appears to have settled down into adulthood as a competent, confident, and responsible young woman. We have what I think is a very good relationship. We see each other frequently, talk about issues in her life, and have genuine affection and love toward one another. We even speak together at a variety of father-daughter events around the country.

I am going to admit right up front that I believe in the old-fashioned notion that a dad should protect his daughter. Our ministry works on a daily basis with too many women, both young and old, who carry the deep wounds from a father who either abandoned them, did not protect them from other males, or did not protect them from life's other cruel intentions. A father should be involved in his daughter's life and the decisions she makes as she approaches adulthood.

Many components of our society would tell you that is a chauvinistic and overbearingly paternalistic way of thinking. They would say that our young women are more liberated and free to disregard this kind of paternal and parental interference—that they are adults and have the right to make their own choices in life. But I say, "Not true." The bane of young women today is that too many fathers have backed away into the shadows and have been "shamed" into being uninvolved in their daughters' lives. This has been destructive to young women on many levels.

A daughter is a gift from God and needs to be treasured, nurtured, and even protected by a father until another man comes along who is qualified to take over that role or until she is mature enough to take over that role herself. That's not to say that women are not equal in every and any way with males; it is merely to say that the powerful influence of a father's love and guidance can make the difference between living a healthy, fulfilling life versus one that is full of hopelessness and despair. Some might argue that women today do not need a man's protection and provision. That may be true, but I would argue just as strongly that daughters do need a father's protection until they reach a stage of maturity when they can fend for themselves.

This book will help fathers understand their daughters on a deep level. It will help them develop the close relationship with their daughters that they each need and crave. Finally, it will help a man understand what his daughter needs from him as a father. I've tried to do this with plainspoken common sense, wisdom, and humor. I've also included some touching stories that will resonate with every father. Many women contributed their stories and experiences to help me explain to you how important a father is to a daughter. Please don't take their input lightly. If you get a chance, read this book with your daughter. I think both men and women will appreciate what they will learn about themselves and their fathers in this book.

1

What Are Little Girls Made Of?

It's your turn to try to quiet the baby. . . . Gently lift the baby to your shoulders. If you're holding baby correctly there should now be vomit on your shoulder. If there is poop on your shoulder, you are holding the baby upside down.

—Dave Barry, advice to new fathers

There's an old nursery rhyme that talks about little girls being made of "sugar and spice and everything nice." Our firstborn, Frank, was a very compliant, easy-to-raise child. Like many families, our second child, Kelsey, was just the opposite. Some might say she was made of "vinegar and vodka and all sorts of drama." It's a common joke around our home that if Kelsey had been born first, Frank might never have been conceived. We would have been scared of having other children. Kelsey is what we call in polite company a "strong-willed" child. She has always had her own mind and her own way of doing things. She frequently did

13

things she knew she shouldn't, despite the consequences involved. In fact, consequences of any kind didn't seem to make a difference once she decided she wanted to do something.

Because of her temperament, Kelsey was a high-maintenance child and took a lot of our attention and resources. For instance, when she was about six years old, she pushed a babysitter down the stairs, and she treed another sitter, who wouldn't come down until we got home. At age two she managed to escape from her crib during naptime, climb up on the stove, and turn all the burners on high. My wife found her sitting and screaming in the middle of the stove between four red-hot burners, her puffy acrylic dress inches from going up in flames.

Once while my wife and I were away, Kelsey "stole" my wife's brand-new sports car and went for a joyride—at age fifteen! Luckily, sibling rivalry was stronger than loyalty, and our son ratted her out with a quick phone call—prompting us to leave for home early. Another time she loaded up our minivan with her "posse" and was involved in an auto accident in a seriously bad part of town. Still another time she was chased down by a baseball-bat-wielding lunatic who smashed out the windshield of our car. Again at age fifteen, she snuck out at 2:30 in the morning once and walked across town to a friend's house—she was gone when we woke up in the morning! I think you get the picture.

One day during Kelsey's tempestuous teenage years, I was talking with a friend. Roger had raised three daughters, and all had been "good" girls who never caused a lick of trouble. They all seemed perfect. Frankly, I was envious of his daughters and not a little concerned about the apparent lack of my own fathering abilities. When I told him about my envy, Roger said something that surprised me. He said, "I know I have been blessed with *good* girls. I think God gave me *good* daughters because he knew I couldn't handle ones who acted out." Perhaps he was only being gracious and was really just a better father than I was, but I like to think perhaps there was some truth in what he said.

Sometimes fathers struggle with feeling inadequate to the task of raising their children. But God chose you to be the father of your daughter despite whatever challenges you think you might have. You are the perfect man to raise your daughter. She has *your* genes in her DNA and *your* blood coursing through her veins. Frankly, God chose you to be your daughter's father despite your inadequacies.

Since information is power, the fact you are reading this book is a good sign that you are a better-than-average father. Be encouraged by the truth that most men feel inadequate at some point during their fatherhood journey. One way to make our job as fathers easier is to understand how and why our girls are the way they are. To do that, let's first look at how they are created. Then we will look at some of the biological differences that make females and males unique. While I doubt many fathers are comfortable thinking about their daughters' reproductive systems or their hormonal stages, I think it is important to set a foundation to build an information base upon. With that in mind, let's look at how she is created and what to expect as she progresses toward womanhood.

Biological and Psychological Makeup

During sexual intercourse, several hundred million sperm are released by the male into the vagina. Sperm travel through the cervix and into the fallopian tubes. If conception takes place, the sperm penetrates an egg and creates a single set of forty-six chromosomes called a zygote, which is the basis for a new human being. The fertilized egg then spends a couple days traveling through the fallopian tube toward the uterus, dividing into cells.[1] It then attaches itself to the lining of the uterus and begins the gestation process.

By eight weeks most of the baby's features are visible. During the first few weeks it is neither male nor female. However, a small group of cells, called the indifferent gonads—which are capable of becoming ovaries or testicles—begin to form. At the same time, other internal features of both sexes develop: the Müllerian ducts (female) and the Wolffian ducts (male). In a female embryo, from about the sixth week, the Wolffian ducts degenerate and the Müllerian ducts develop toward the fallopian tubes, uterus, and vagina. Meanwhile, by the twelfth week, the indifferent gonads begin to develop into ovaries.[2]

Shortly after birth, subtle behavioral differences between boy and girl babies begin to appear. These differences are likely caused by a combination of natural (biological) and nurture (socialization) factors. In general,

> boys tend to be more active, while girls are more verbal. A Canadian study shows that boys tend to be more aggressive on the outside, while girls practice mental and emotional aggression instead.
>
> Girls and women also tend to be more empathetic, more ready to share their emotions, and they have a better awareness about their environment. The differences in empathy grow with age as girls develop stronger communication skills and develop stronger intimate friendships that often last for years. . . .
>
> Females score higher in skills related to speaking, reading, writing, and spelling, while boys have a better spatial imagination. In studies, boys were able to mentally rotate objects better than 80% of the girls.[3]

Not surprisingly, because of this aptitude, more boys than girls tend to be attracted to subjects like engineering and architecture.[4]

Until about the age of eight, girls are not significantly different in their physiological makeup than boys. That all changes with the onset of puberty, which is discussed in detail below. One area, though, that we should be aware of is how our perception of our daughters changes once they enter puberty.

By puberty, many parents (with the encouragement of our culture) think that teenagers are just young adults, capable of making informed and intelligent decisions on their own. While late adolescence is a time to help them develop these skills, the truth is that the decision-making part of the brain—the prefrontal cortex—is not fully developed until about the midtwenties. The prefrontal cortex is the part of the brain responsible for reasoning, critical thinking skills, impulse control, and sound judgment. So when we send our young people off to college at age eighteen and expect them to make good decisions, we may have unrealistic expectations. Truthfully, even if they want to make good choices, they may not have the capability. That doesn't excuse them for making bad choices; it only provides a possible explanation.

Additionally, teens are developing critical thinking skills and understanding concepts they previously did not comprehend. They grow cognitively with the ability to grasp abstract thoughts, think into the future, and develop moral reasoning. Both my son and daughter went through legalistic, argumentative stages while they were developing their abstract intelligence. Sometimes—no, most of the time—it drove me crazy!

Puberty

Adolescence (beginning with puberty) may be the most challenging time in a girl's life. She experiences a roller coaster of physical and emotional changes, and she begins placing a high importance on being accepted by others and achieving society's illusive standard of beauty.

From the moment she is born, your little baby girl is striving toward adulthood. Your little girl *will* become a woman, and it *will* seem like it happened sooner than you expected when it becomes a reality. Even as you read this book, her body is creeping (and sometimes rushing) toward that goal. One day her body will explode into womanhood, and you will be faced with challenges you never thought possible. If you're like most fathers, this change will catch you off guard. It will be confusing, frustrating, and even a little frightening.

Puberty often starts at about age nine in girls. Puberty marks the beginning of adolescence and is a time when hormones increase and cause changes to her body. Her breasts develop and her hips widen. She gains height and weight, develops pubic hair, and starts menstruating (having her period). Her female reproductive organs mature and her body becomes ready for reproduction. As her reproductive organs mature, she can now become pregnant. The pituitary gland controls all of these changes, causing the ovaries to produce the female sex hormones that launch her into womanhood.[5] As her body develops, she may look like a full-grown woman, but inside she is likely still a little girl.

These changes can cause unexpected consequences. Kelsey was always a gifted athlete growing up. She played soccer and basketball from age five up through high school. I'm convinced she could have gotten college scholarships in either sport, but she chose not to go that route. One of her advantages was she was always faster than her competitors. I remember a soccer game in about eighth grade. I was commenting to another father how much faster she used to be when she was younger. I couldn't figure out why she couldn't run as fast as she used to—I thought perhaps she was not trying very hard. A nearby mom overheard our conversation and politely told me that my daughter had gone through puberty and now had breasts and hips, so of course she couldn't run as fast anymore. That thought had never occurred to me until then.

Hormones

Have you noticed any of the following behaviors in your teenage daughter:

instantaneous mood changes
taking things personally
a drop in self-esteem

hypersensitivity to what others say

not liking herself

trouble concentrating

difficulty making decisions

Family therapist Michael Gurian says, "If you noticed any of these or other symptoms of possible mood disorder or bipolar disorder, you've just described a normal adolescent girl."[6]

Teenage girls can be temperamental. As the great philosopher Curly Howard once said, "I'm temperamental—95 percent temper and 5 percent mental! Nyuk, nyuk, nyuk." That describes many girls during adolescence. One man told me, "My daughter changed dramatically at about thirteen years old. She used to think I was wonderful. But almost overnight I went from a guy who could do no wrong to a guy who could do no right. Suddenly I was a loser."

These symptoms are caused by the complexity of the female monthly cycle and the effects of a greater variety of hormones than males experience. Chemical imbalances in young females can cause drastic changes in their personalities and behaviors. Basically, hormones tell the millions of cells in a girl's body what to do, when to do it, and how it looks. They affect her mood, her appetite, her communication style, her self-image and self-esteem, and her primary emotions (anger, joy, grief). This interaction is all very complex, but here's a short summary of the most powerful hormones that influence your daughter.

Estrogen is a family of hormones that are the primary female hormone. They are the most influential hormone of a girl's physical, mental, and emotional experiences. Estrogen has been likened to "one of the most dominant forces on earth."[7] Estrogen controls the amount of norepinephrine, serotonin, prolactin, and dopamine, which in turn control mood stability, thought process, perception, memory, personal motivation, anxiety, stress, and sex drive in a female. This hormone powerfully affects the mood of a girl and her yearning for intimacy.[8]

Progesterone is another major hormone in females. Progesterone rises during the monthly cycle, shutting down estrogen levels. This often causes girls to feel withdrawn, irritable, and depressed. Progesterone is called the "bonding" hormone. Besides bonding fertilized eggs to the walls of the uterus, it also helps create complex social bonding structures when mixed with other chemicals like oxytocin. This is why females are often more nurturing and better caregivers than males. It is why families and relationships are so important to them. Estrogen and progesterone both need to be in delicate balance for a girl to feel balanced.[9]

Testosterone is also present in females, although to a much lesser extent than in adolescent males. Higher levels of testosterone in both males and females relates to less depression, more aggression, and a greater sex drive.

Your daughter's emotional state (her feelings) are a direct result of the influence of her hormones. These hormones cause her to want stronger and deeper personal relationships, more intimate friendships, and greater bonding attachments, and to have more compassion and empathy for others.

Let's take a break from hormones and look at a couple other developmental factors to be aware of.

Brain Works

There's a lot more going on inside your daughter's head than you can possibly imagine. As men, we tend to think in a structured, logical, and linear process. But her mind encompasses every detail of the world around her. Every emotion she feels and that anyone around her is feeling is part of this process. There are hundreds of thoughts, ideas, feelings, and imaginings all happening at once in her mind, some of them in conflict with each other.

A big complaint from girls to their parents is, "You don't understand me," or "You really don't know me." They may have a point. Fathers and brothers typically think of teen girls as alien beings. And moms seem to have forgotten what they felt like at that age. I asked my wife many times when our daughter was going through puberty, "What in the world is she thinking?" Even though she had been a young woman once, my wife claimed to have no knowledge of our daughter's thought process. Frankly, most girls don't know or understand themselves, which makes it even more frustrating that no one else can tell them what is going on and why they act like they do.

> **Letters from Kelsey (age 15)**
>
> Hey Daddy,
>   Happy birthday! 48 wow! You're old . . . er than me! Yeah, I know I've been acting weird lately, but I still love you a lot! I may not "show it" like other people or I may not say it as much as I should, but still know that I do love you! I like the fact that you're doing this Better Dads thing, it's just one more thing about you that makes me proud to have you as my daddy. I'll love you always n forever, Kelsey Johnson (your only daughter).

For most of humankind's history the female brain was equipped for taking care of children, requiring the development of emotive skills. In contrast, male brains developed mainly for hunting and other spatial activities like building and designing. The female brain, though, concentrated on processing the "emotional core" of the object she interacted with. Constant and intensive child care—as well as hands-on care of the sick, elderly, and disadvantaged—propels a brain structure to evolve toward in-depth emotive processing.[10]

A female brain develops areas that allow earlier language skills, verbal skills, and memory retention than males. Michael Gurian says, "The female brain, however, is coded to grow more quickly from right to left than the male. This is one of the reasons that female children, at very young ages, already use a higher quantity of words and more coherent language than boys. They speak, in general, earlier than boys. The left hemisphere, where most language takes place, develops earlier in girls."[11]

The female brain also produces more serotonin, which relates to greater impulse control. This is one reason why young girls can remain calmer than young boys do in the same situations. The female brain secretes more oxytocin than a male's. This means she has a greater capacity to care and nurture others. When a girl hears a baby cry, her body releases oxytocin, which produces a maternal instinct and causes her to want to hold the baby (which then causes more oxytocin to be released).

Even the way a female is wired biologically contributes to this nurturing ability. Researchers at the University of Pennsylvania performed magnetic resonance imaging (MRI) brain scans on men and women. The experimenters induced stress in the subjects by having them count backward as quickly as possible from 1,600 by 13. Imaging showed that while under stress more blood flow went to the prefrontal cortex in men, the area of the brain that induces a fight-or-flight response. In women, more blood flow went to the limbic system of the brain, the area responsible for "tend and befriend" or nurturing behavior.[12]

A girl's sense of touch, hearing, and smell is greater than a boy's. She has a greater capacity to want to touch something for longer periods of time, deriving joy from the contact. She is creating an inner world that is much more sense- and contact-oriented than a boy's.[13] Since the vast majority of brain growth occurs during the first five years of a child's life, this is the best time to lay a foundation for a girl's life. This is a time when we need to protect her brain from harmful media messages, dangerous people, and bad influences. During this period, be sure to give her continual physical and emotional bonding.

As a girl gets older, other areas of her brain will begin to develop and you'll notice significant changes. For example, due to a larger hippocampus and the greater number and speed of neuron transmissions, girls typically have a greater memory capacity than boys do. By age eight or nine, most girls can complete a list of chores without being reminded, while boys typically cannot.

During adolescence, a girl will experience another rapid growth pattern within her brain. Puberty releases hormones that create a positive "neurologically traumatic crisis" within her brain.[14] These dramatic changes can be confusing and frightening to a girl (and her father).

The ten- to twelve-year-old stage appears to be relatively significant in the brain development of girls. Brain growth during these years allows her to take on new skills, insights, abstract concepts, and abilities to think and argue. By twelve, many of the things she has learned will stick with her the rest of her life. Gurian says,

> A girl's relationships, intimacies, sports activities, art and musical activities, as well as academic learning during the ten-to-twelve period have a greater likelihood of "sticking" or at least "reappearing" later in her life because of their interconnection with the massive brain growth. . . . This is why, generally, we can say that if she enjoys piano at eleven, she'll probably remain somewhat musical during her life. If she reads a lot at twelve, she'll probably enjoy reading throughout life. If she's in stable relationships at ten, she'll probably feel safer in stable relationships throughout life.[15]

Girls at this age tend to struggle with making decisions. Their brains, on average, are taking in more data and input to more *parts* of the brain than boys' brains are. Hence, boys tend to be single-task oriented, while girls agonize over five or ten elements of even a small decision. Frequently adolescent girls find it easier to let someone else make a decision for them than to think everything through and make no decision at all.

During the rapid brain growth that occurs throughout adolescence, our daughters actually need *more* guidance, input, and stability rather than less. This can be challenging because this is a time when a girl is seeking more independence and does not want her father telling her what to do. But the truth is she needs you more now than she probably did even as a young girl.

Genetic Influences

One area that we tend to overlook in the development of our children is the importance of genetic influences, especially when compared to the environmental influences in their lives. I'm not a particularly big proponent of either the nurture or nature theory being exclusive in a person's development. I think most of us are a combination of both our genetic makeup and the environment we were raised in.

Recently, however, I have become more aware of the powerful influence our genetic code plays in our personal development. One rather humorous example of this is the similarities between my biological father and myself. I first met him when I was twenty-four years old. We look alike and stand with the same posture, and over the years, our wives have delighted in the fact that we also have a predisposition for the same clothing, foods, sleeping style, and many other habits and behaviors. When my dad and his wife drove up from California to visit us, we both were wearing the exact same unique brown velour shirt (there were probably only two of them in the entire country). Clearly, since I was never influenced by him as a child, these idiosyncrasies are the result of genetic coding that somehow determines my unconscious behavior, choices, and preferences in life.

But I have noticed even more destructive types of behaviors attributed to some form of genetic imprint. Most of us are aware of the generational cycles (or sins) that occur in families. Oftentimes these occur from modeled behaviors, but I'm convinced many are also derived (or at least influenced) from our genetic makeup. Modeled behaviors, especially from primary caretakers, *are* a hugely powerful indicator in our own behavioral outcomes. We often see generations of families where alcoholism, abandonment, or abusive behavior that was modeled by parents is emulated and passed down from one generation to the next. However, genetics also appears to play a significant role in our outcomes, especially if we are unaware of its influence.

I have observed this in many of the population we work with in our ministry. For example, virtually every female in every generation of one young woman's family—for as far back as anyone can remember—has been an unwed teenage mother. Even females who had been adopted out of the biological family followed this genetic blueprint for their lives. Knowing this predilection, her mother and father were determined to break this cycle with their daughter. However, despite raising her in a relatively healthy two-parent environment, being aware of the challenges they faced, and talking with her about those challenges, it took all of their mightiest efforts to keep that genetic legacy from coming to fruition. It was almost as if she was predisposed to make choices that forced her to accomplish the genetic coding in her DNA. She was prone to make self-destructive decisions and have attitudes that reflected those of the women in her family of origin, even though she had not been exposed to that kind of behavior.

This phenomenon is also observed in adopted children who act out in behaviors (substance abuse, promiscuity, out-of-wedlock childbirth) similar to their birth parents even having never met them. Certainly there are other factors involved in the behaviors of adopted children, not the least of which involves issues of abandonment, but many children raised in healthy adoptive families make destructive life choices eerily similar to those that their birth parents engaged in, even though they may not have any awareness of those behaviors.

I believe wholeheartedly that the models we are raised with while growing up are the biggest influences in the way we learn to live our lives. But perhaps more often than we recognize, we are "preprogrammed" or predisposed to make choices that result in outcomes with a basis in our "generational heritage." Being conscious of these historical tendencies allows us to make intentional choices to break generational influences instead of inadvertently falling into a preordained future.

As an example, if the women in your heritage have had problems with addictions or alcoholism, your daughter has a greater likelihood of being attracted to these substances.

We find that education is the first step to breaking generational cycles. Making your daughter aware of genetic propensities can go a long way to helping her avoid those traps. It also helps *you* not get blindsided by some tragedy that comes out of the blue. Other things like mental illness, diseases, depression, and eating disorders also have genetic components associated with them.

Look at your and your wife's heritage closely. See if there are specific cycles that present themselves throughout generations that need to be addressed. Many men are caught off guard by not being aware of potential potholes in the genetic coding passed on to their daughters. It's not that your daughter is predestined to act this way, but it may be something you need to be aware of in order to develop a comprehensive plan to raise her into healthy adulthood.

Menstrual Cycle

Until menopause, all women (and girls going through puberty) are subject to a hormonal cycle each month (or every twenty-eight days on average). For most men, this process is mysterious and more than a little scary. Most of us feel this subject is strictly on a "need to know" basis, and we don't want too much information. But as much as I don't want to think about this in relation to my daughter, I believe it is important for us to have more than just superficial knowledge in order to understand what changes the women in our lives go through each month.

Understanding this cycle may help explain many behaviors of women that are confusing to most men. So here is a quick primer on a woman's menstrual cycle.

Baby girls are born with ovaries, fallopian tubes, and a uterus. The two ovaries contain thousands of eggs. Each fallopian tube stretches from an ovary to the uterus. As a girl matures and enters puberty, the pituitary gland releases hormones that stimulate the ovaries to produce estrogen and progesterone. These hormones have many effects on a girl's body, including her physical maturation, growth, and emotions.

About once a month, a tiny egg leaves one of the ovaries and travels down one of the fallopian tubes toward the uterus. In the days before ovulation, the hormone estrogen stimulates the uterus to build up its lining with extra blood and tissue, making the walls of the uterus thick and cushioned. This prepares the uterus for pregnancy. If the egg is fertilized by a sperm cell, it travels to the uterus and attaches to the cushiony wall of the uterus, where it slowly develops into a baby.

If the egg isn't fertilized—which is the case during most of a woman's monthly cycles—it doesn't attach to the wall of the uterus. When this happens, the uterus sheds the extra lining. The blood, tissue, and unfertilized egg leave the uterus, going through the vagina on the way out of the body. This is a menstrual period. This cycle happens almost every month for several more decades (except, of course, during pregnancy) until a woman reaches menopause and no longer releases eggs from her ovaries.[16] Most menstrual periods last from three to seven days. Body chemicals (hormones) rise and fall—sometimes dramatically—during the month to make the menstrual cycle happen.[17]

Many females experience symptoms associated with premenstrual syndrome (PMS), a normal part of the cycle process. One type of PMS is characterized by anxiety, irritability, and mood swings. Most likely, this type of PMS relates to the balance between estrogen and progesterone produced in the body. If estrogen predominates, anxiety occurs. If there's more progesterone, depression may be a complaint.

Sugar craving, fatigue, and headaches signify a different type of PMS. In addition to sugar, women may crave chocolate, white bread, white rice, pastries, and noodles. (Judging from these symptoms, I frequently suffer from PMS.) These food cravings may be caused by the increased responsiveness to insulin related to increased hormone levels before menstruation. In this circumstance, women may experience symptoms of low blood sugar; their brains are signaling a need for fuel. A consistent diet that includes complex carbohydrates will provide a steady flow of energy to the brain and counter the ups and downs of blood sugar variations.[18]

Uterine cramping is one of the most common uncomfortable sensations women may have during menstruation. There are two kinds of cramping. Spasmodic cramping is probably caused by chemicals that affect muscle tension. Some of these chemicals cause relaxation, and some cause constriction. The other type, congestive cramping, causes the body to retain fluids and salt. Other symptoms of PMS include acne, bloating, weight gain, tender or swollen breasts, cramping, constipation, nausea, and mood swings. Additionally, there are several complications that can make menstruation very painful for women or girls. Premenstrual water retention is a phenomenon that accompanies menstruation for many women. Water retention makes women feel bloated. It can cause uncomfortable swelling in the breasts, swelling in the feet or ankles, and a bloated stomach.

With all this complicated activity going on, it makes me pretty glad I'm a man.

Hormonal Influences

The hormone fluctuations a woman experiences frequently cause her to act easily hurt, angry, irritable, unreasonable, or illogical at times. I don't know whether or not this cycle contributes to or promotes disharmony in the home, but I have my suspicions. I haven't done any scientific studies to confirm my theory, but after having a wife and a teenage daughter in the house together, I do know there were specific times each month when things seemed pretty chaotic and frazzled around the home front. Much like coming face-to-face with a brown bear in the wilderness, there have been times where I had to follow the "Do not make eye contact—back away slowly" strategy to escape physical harm. Real or perceived slights and hurts were magnified, and expectations seemed unrealistic (at least to me and my son). The women in our home were irritable, easily hurt and offended, defensive, and downright angry during this time. They acted illogically, irrationally, and even appeared to suffer from temporary insanity. It's no mystery to me why ancient tribes used to segregate women from the clan during this time of the month.

Just recently I made the mistake of mentioning that a particular blouse my wife had bought was less than flattering on her—it made her look heavier than she actually was. You'd think after thirty years or so I'd be smart enough to know better. I thought I was doing her a favor by mentioning this just before we went out to dinner, because she had previously gotten mad at me for *not* mentioning that an article of clothing didn't look good on her. She had recently lost a lot of weight and looked really good. I didn't think she would want to wear something unflattering. Once I had reattached my head after having it bitten off, I was pretty confused about what I'm supposed to do and what I'm not supposed to say (not to mention when to say it).

A recent study conducted on the neurochemistry of the brain during menstruation shows there may be some significant biological causes for a woman's erratic behavior. Using a technique called functional magnetic resonance imaging (MRI), the scientists looked at blood oxygen patterns in women's brains at two stages of their monthly cycle: just before menstruation and around a week after. The scans showed that all of the women in the experiment had more electrical activity in the frontal lobe of the brain during the

29

premenstrual period, the time when most women might experience PMS.

Most often when PMS was present, they saw dramatic differences between the scans. They found that "when a woman feels good, her deep limbic system is calm and cool and she has good activity in her temporal lobes and prefrontal cortex. Right before her period, when she feels the worst, her deep limbic system is often overactive and she has poor activity in her temporal lobes and prefrontal cortex!"[19]

The study noted two distinct PMS patterns that respond to different treatments. One pattern involved increased deep limbic activity often accompanied by excessive activity in the temporal lobe. This activity "correlates with cyclic mood changes. When the limbic system is more active on the left side it is often associated with anger, irritability, and expressed negative emotion. When it is more active on the right side it is often associated with sadness, emotional withdrawal, anxiety, and repressed negative emotion. Left-sided abnormalities are more of a problem for other people (outwardly directed anger and irritability), while right-sided overactivity is more of an internal problem."[20]

The second PMS pattern noted was "increased deep limbic activity in conjunction with increased cingulate gyrus activity. This area is the part of the brain associated with shifting attention. Women with this pattern often complain of increased sadness, worrying, repetitive negative thoughts, and verbalizations (nagging) and cognitive inflexibility."[21]

Okay, you can stop and take a deep breath now. Now that the uncomfortable stuff is over with, let's look at some topics that are easier to think about regarding our daughters.

FOR DISCUSSION AND REFLECTION

• Establish habits with your daughter when she is young, and this will serve your relationship well later in life—habits such as spending time with her, listening to her, and communicating effectively. What are some activities you can do together as part of "your" time that can become part of your relationship legacy? What are some ways you can be intentional about listening to and talking with her on a daily basis?

- To prepare for the physical, psychological, and emotional changes that will take place in your daughter during puberty, familiarize yourself with the biological changes and the effects that hormones have on your daughter's body. Develop a "game plan" or strategy before she enters puberty so that you are prepared for those changes and challenges.

2

Her Father's Influence

It is from her father that she begins to infer messages that will linger a lifetime—"I am, or am not, considered by men to be pretty, desirable, valuable, dependent, weak, strong, dim-witted, brilliant"; "Men are, or are not, trustworthy, loving, predatory, dependable, available, dangerous."

—Victoria Secunda, *Women and Their Fathers*

Fathers have been given a tremendous ability to influence the lives of their daughters. This incredible paternal influence was once illustrated to me very powerfully. My office is in our family room, where the television is also located (probably not the wisest choice). One day Kelsey was home sick from school and was watching a program on television about training young women how to become models. On this episode, as part of their training, the young women—hoping to become famous models—were taking acting lessons. The acting teacher was instructing the girls how to cry on command. She gave each girl a blank piece of paper and told her to imagine that it was a note from her father saying he was leaving her forever and never wanted to see her again. Every one of the young women instantly burst into tears, some of them sobbing in anguish.

After a few minutes of crying and hugging one another, the girls were then told by the instructor to rip up the paper and release their anger at their fathers. These young women ferociously tore into the papers with almost violent anger. It was a stunning illustration of a father's importance to a daughter. Either these young women were already the best actresses I've ever seen, or it was a gripping testament to the role a father plays in the life of a woman.

In preparation for writing this book, I asked dozens of women about the relationship they had with their father and the impact he had on their life. I wish I could say that they were all heroic and uplifting stories, but the truth is many of them were devastating tales of deeply wounded women who made terrible choices in an effort to try and fill the void in their soul that their father left unfulfilled.

The Power of a Father

Fathers have an incredible influence (positive or negative) on nearly every aspect of their daughters' lives. Because a daughter so yearns to secure the love of her father, she believes what her father believes about her. If he calls her stupid or incompetent, she will believe that about herself. If he labels her plain-Jane or worthless or inept, she will have a hard time believing anything different about herself as a woman. But if he calls her intelligent, beautiful, competent, and accomplished, then she will believe that to be true. A father determines how a girl feels about herself.

Author and pediatrician Meg Meeker describes the yearning daughters have for the approval of their fathers:

> And I have watched daughters talk to their fathers. When you come in the room, they change. Everything about them changes: their eyes, their mouths, their gestures, their body language. Daughters are never lukewarm in the presence of their fathers. They might take their mothers for granted, but not you. They light up—or they cry. They watch you intensely. They hang on your words. They hope for your attention, and they wait for it in frustration—or in despair. They need a gesture of approval, a nod of encouragement, or even a simple eye contact to let them know you care and are willing to help.[1]

Fathers have a huge impact on the intellectual, emotional, and physical development of their daughters as well. Toddlers with father attachments have better problem-solving skills.[2] Girls with close father relationships achieve higher academic success.[3] As a girl gets older, father-connectedness is the number one factor in delaying and preventing her from engaging in premarital sex and drug and alcohol abuse. Girls with involved fathers are more assertive and have higher self-esteem.[4] And girls with involved fathers also have higher quantitative and verbal skills and higher intellectual functioning.[5]

As a man and a father I'm pretty sure I did not recognize the power I had in my daughter's life. Yes, I probably knew on some level that I was important. But I never knew *how* important my approval and love at such a visceral level were to my daughter. If I had, I would have been much more intentional in the way I spoke to her and more aware of the messages I was really speaking into her heart. In fact, guys, if you want to understand your wife better, I suggest you look at the relationship she has or had with her father.

You can tell the endearment that women hold for their fathers merely by how they address them. For most women, her father is the most important male in her life. Girls usually stop calling their mothers "Mommy" sometime around the age of eight or nine. But many grown women still call their fathers "Daddy."[6] Lois Mowday says in her book *Daughters without Dads*, "Daddy, for the little girl, is the final authority in approving or disapproving who she is. Many women admitted to me that they had enjoyed a fair amount of affirmation from various people. But if their fathers displayed disapproval, it was as if all the other approval didn't even count. They needed the final okay from daddy."[7]

A Father's Words

A father's spoken or written words contain great power. A man's hurtful spoken words can cripple his child's soul for life. Many women cherish notes or other blessings they've received from their fathers. Sometimes these words seem inconsequential to us and yet are treasures to our daughters. One woman spoke of a paper-coated clothes hanger that was her most cherished possession. Her father had written "I love you" on it when she was a little girl. She carried it with her all through college and into her marriage. Elderly people have told me their only regret in life was that they never heard their father say "I'm proud of you" or "I love you."

Most important is for you to make sure your daughter knows you love her. Because females are more verbally oriented than males, they place a higher value on words than the average male does. Consequently, a daughter has a powerful need to *hear* her worth from the important men in her life. She derives her self-esteem and value from what her father speaks into her heart (more on that later).

God has placed within a daughter's heart the inherent desire, even *need*, to love and respect her father. Even people who have been abused or abandoned by their fathers still *want* to love and respect them. Many girls with fathers in prison still hold them up on a pedestal and refuse to acknowledge their failings. Again, this is a huge power that as fathers and men we need to recognize and treat with respect.

Role Model of Manhood

A father sets a huge role model for his daughter regarding the qualities she looks for in men and the standards she maintains. He is the first man in her life and models how a man should treat a woman, how a man should act, and how a man shows healthy love and affection to a woman. He also sets the standard for how a daughter feels she deserves to be treated by men. He even determines how a girl feels about herself. If a father shows his daughter love, respect, and appreciation for who she is, she will believe that about herself as a woman, no matter what anyone else thinks. Dads who model a strong work ethic show young girls how men are supposed to provide for their families.

A little girl who has her father's love knows what it's like to be unconditionally and completely adored by a man. She knows the feeling of safety that love creates.[8] As author Dr. Kevin Leman says, "The father-daughter relationship is the key to every woman's aching heart. It's the genesis of every grown woman's sighs. It's also, unfortunately, the missing ingredient in many lost souls."[9]

You are her first love. Every man in her life will be compared to you, whether consciously or unconsciously. A girl's father shapes her relationship with every other male she meets in life. As one young woman said, "My father's model of integrity was what I used to judge other men with. Without it I wouldn't have known what to look for in a man and I wouldn't have recognized it when I saw it even if I had."

A father also sets the standards a woman expects to live her life by. A woman named Mary told me, "My dad taught me to value honesty, hard work, education, and independence. I tend to have high expectations of myself because I always tried to do better for myself, but also for my dad so he would say he was proud of me. I also tend to expect others to live up to my standards and expectations."

Conversely, men who abandon or abuse their daughters set them up for a lifetime of pain, distrust, and feelings of worthlessness. You can feel the pain in this woman's statement: "I have expectations of being special, loved, cared for, and protected that my spouse is not able to live up to. I grew up feeling angry, unloved, unappreciated, not accepted. I know my value, but I struggle with believing that others know my value, even God."

When men are angry or disrespectful toward the females in their families, it sets their daughters up to expect this kind of treatment from men. If a man does not provide for and protect his daughter, she has no expectations of this behavior from the men she enters into relationships with. Why would a woman willingly marry a man who can't or won't hold a job to support his family? Why would she intentionally marry a man who abuses her? She probably wouldn't. Perhaps that was the type of man that was modeled for her growing up, and she is subconsciously attracted to that model, believing she deserves that kind of treatment and is unworthy of anything better.

A father's model even influences how a woman feels about women in general. Dr. Leman explains it this way:

> Women who have a low view of women invariably marry men with a low view of women. Ironically, it takes a strong father to give a woman a high view of femininity. Kids—especially daughters—get a sense from their dads that they're worth being loved. The woman who doesn't have a good self-image because she had no father or had a non-affirming father will typically marry a non-husband or a non-affirming husband.[10]

When dad is not around to provide a model of masculinity or to nurture his daughter's soul, the consequences can be devastating to girls and young women.

The Effects of Fatherlessness on Girls

What happens when Dad isn't in his daughter's life? Does he still influence her in every area of life? Remember that a man does not have to be physically absent for a girl to be fatherless. He can also be emotionally, spiritually, and psychologically absent (or abusive) and can still wreak the same havoc in his daughter's life by his noninvolvement.

The truth is that a father's influence is so powerful on his children that even his absence affects them. In fact, one of the more accurate ways to measure the power of something is to look at what happens when it is absent.

Girls without fathers are much more likely to engage in early sexually promiscuous behavior, become unwed teenage mothers, drop out of high school, and suffer lower educational outcomes. They are also subject to a variety of other risk factors—such as poverty; physical, emotional, and psychological abuse; drug and alcohol use; and crime—that attribute to a poorer quality of life.[11]

But beyond the physical risks, girls without fathers suffer psychological disadvantages as well. A common theme among women who did not have a father is the inability to trust a man and to believe that he won't eventually abandon her. There is a deep anger toward men by women whose fathers have abandoned or wounded them. Counting on and loving a man is a leap of faith, because for them a permanent relationship with a man is entirely theoretical. These women tend to test the men in their lives by starting fights, finding flaws, or expecting to be abandoned.[12]

One woman who grew up fatherless readily admitted to me that she spent many years pushing her husband as far as she could just to test him and make sure he wouldn't leave her. Her fear of abandonment nearly drove her into a self-fulfilling prophecy.

Even girls whose fathers have failed them continue to yearn for his love and affection. You can hear the anguish of failed expectations in this woman's voice:

My father divorced my mother when I was seven years old. Because he constantly failed me while growing up, I had hardened my heart and finally cut him out of my life completely. Two years later I was pregnant and went into labor. I'm in the delivery room waiting to dilate enough to push and I look over at my mom and almost in a childlike voice I say to her, "Call my daddy." My mom thought I was joking. I told her I was not joking. I wanted her to call him and tell him I was in labor and that I needed him there. She called him. He said he was on his way to the hospital. He never showed up. I think for a brief moment in time that "little girl" in me yearned for her daddy, regardless of the twenty-five years of heartache he had put me through. Sadly, I knew the whole time he would never show up. I hoped he would but knew he wouldn't. Kind of like all the years as a child when he would say he was in town and would stop by. I would put my best outfit on and sit by the picture window of our house waiting for hours, hoping he would show but knowing he wouldn't.

Girls who do not receive healthy masculine love and affection from their fathers have a craving for it throughout their lives. Many women either willingly substitute or confuse sex for love in their desire for masculine affection. As one woman described it, "Daughters who sleep around never understand that the hole in their hearts they are trying to fill with sex is a hole that their fathers never filled with the cement of love and faithfulness." As I think back to when I was young, all of the girls available for sexual favors came from either fatherless or abusive backgrounds. Of course, the young men who took advantage of them did not recognize it as such, merely as opportunity.

Daughters who have had the benefit of healthy father involvement are more independent and self-possessed, and they are more likely to assume responsibility for the consequences of their actions. Father-deprived girls show precocious sexual interest (they are three times more likely to become pregnant out of wedlock than their fathered counterparts) and have less ability to maintain sexual and emotional adjustments with just one male. Without a father, a girl must learn about boys without a man's perspective. She is like a lamb without a shepherd. Without a father's influence and guidance, even the most normal male activities may seem bizarre and strange to her.

Author and speaker Angela Thomas says, "I can be in a small group of women and tell you in a matter of moments which ones have had a healthy, loving relationship with their fathers. There is a certain confidence and peace that comes from a woman who has known such love. And there is an anxiousness and insecurity buried inside a woman who has never known a father's love or, worse, who has suffered wounds from his words or his distance or his hands."[13] Women who have been hurt deeply in some way by their fathers tend to either take that pain out on men throughout their lifetimes or become victims of men.

Without a father around to provide a role model, healthy physical affection, and protection, a girl is left to the examples of manhood she sees on television, in the movies, and in music videos—by all accounts very poor options. Fathers can act as filters for much of the noise our culture throws at girls—without that filter girls are stressed and bewildered. They are left to the mercy of the young men (many of whom never had fathers either) who prowl around like packs of wolves. Males have an internal radar that can detect female sexual availability or vulnerability. This exposes young girls and women to predators who prey upon them and manipulate their unconscious desire and yearning for father-love. Combine this with a girl's natural longing for an older male's physical and emotional affection, and we see an increase in unwed teenage mothers, per-petuating the cycle anew. Many fatherless girls fall for the first male who shows them any kind of affection or attention that they crave.

Without a model of how a woman and man interact together, a girl is left on her own to learn about the mysterious and frightening world of males—she doesn't have the real thing at home to watch and examine. One fatherless woman told me, "I was fascinated by men. I wanted to please them, therefore I compromised some of my values." Another stated, "I was begging for any man to love me. I never believed anyone would love me if they knew me. I sought any attention I could from men—time, touch, promises." And still another described it this way: "I tend to be drawn to any man who pays attention to me. I feel flattered and surprised by the attention. I guess I sell myself short."

Any child deprived of his or her God-given right to a father suffers from father hunger. Both boys and girls suffer from this father hunger, yet each expresses it differently as adults. Your daughter needs you in her life, no matter how young or old she is.

Your Relationship with Her Mother

Perhaps the greatest gift you can give your daughter is to show her how a man loves a woman—model how she should expect to be treated and loved by a man. Just as fathers are the biggest influences as role models regarding masculinity for their sons, so too are mothers the greatest role models of femininity for their daughters. A mother teaches what a woman's roles are in life, how to fulfill those roles, and what healthy femininity looks like. A mother also models to her daughter how to love a man, what level of respect men deserve, and what a woman's role is in marriage. A happy, secure, and confident wife teaches her daughters good things about men and relationships.

Abraham Lincoln is credited with saying, "The greatest gift a man can give his children is to love their mother." Your daughter is watching to see how she should expect to be treated by her future boyfriends and husband. Teach your daughter that she should *expect* to be treated with respect by other males. I see so many girls and women who allow themselves to be treated poorly by the men in their lives. The way a man treats his wife speaks volumes to a girl on how she should expect to be treated and valued by men later in her life. If her father shows that he values her mother as someone worthy of love and respect, a girl will expect that from her husband (or boyfriends). But if he exhibits a model of abuse or disrespect for her mother, a girl may feel that she deserves to be treated that way as a wife as well.

The other day I was resting on a bench, enjoying the sunshine during my daily summer bike ride. From about fifty yards away, I could hear some people coming down the path. As they got closer, I could see a young woman striding purposefully, followed about ten feet behind by what I gathered was her boyfriend. Both were in their late teens or early twenties. She was fairly attractive while he was tall, skinny, tattooed, and unshaven, with pants sagging below his underwear. They were obviously having a disagreement and were sniping at each other as they walked along the trail. After they had passed by me about thirty yards down the lane, I heard him call her a filthy name and say, "You're lucky I don't smash your face into the concrete!" My first sad thought was, *Who taught them that was an acceptable way to communicate? And why did the girl think that she deserved to be spoken to like that?* Had either or both of them had that behavior modeled for them by a father or father figure? Or had one or both of their mothers allowed themselves to be spoken to like that?

Fathering expert Dr. Ken Canfield says,

> All children are born as bachelors and bachelorettes. The first impression they have of marriage is what they observe in their own parents' union. They're watching you. They're taking notes. Your sons, however subconsciously, are asking the question: What does it mean to be a husband? They are also trying to figure out who these creatures called women are, and they are looking to you to see how you perceive them and what respect you give to them. Your daughters also have their eye on you. To submit to another in the mystery of marriage can be a fearful thing; your daughters are asking themselves how well their mother fared in the deal.[14]

Your daughter needs to see you praise your wife on a daily basis. Your praise means more to your wife than anyone else's. She needs to be constantly reminded how important she is in the lives of her family. Her role is often a thankless one that does not receive the accolades of our culture. Her maternal role as nurturer and helpmate provides vital support to your role as provider and leader of your family.

Bill Bright, founder of Campus Crusade, said,

> If a woman is beautiful in her teens and twenties, it's because God made her that way. But after she's married and the years pass, if she's still beautiful when she's fifty, sixty, and seventy years old, it's because of the way her husband treats her. So men, take another look at your wife. If for some reason she is dowdy and glum and depressed and discouraged, look in the mirror, and see who is the major contributor to her looks. Then cultivate her with love. Before long that dull countenance will become radiant and filled with joy.[15]

Tell your wife in front of your daughter every day that you love her, and spend time praising her for her good attributes. Tell her you appreciate her when she does something for you. Don't just comment when she disappoints you. Look for opportunities to use the power God has given you to lift her up to be the maximum woman God intended her to be. When your daughter sees those actions modeled, she will internalize them as how a woman should be treated.

As we will discuss throughout this book, a father also contributes to the kind of man his daughter will marry or be attracted to. Dr. Leman says this about a father's influence in this area:

> If you act like a controlling, demanding, and lazy bum, your daughter won't think it odd or undesirable when she dates a boy who treats her this way. The best thing you can do to shape your daughter's view of men is to treat your wife like you want your future son-in-law to treat your daughter. More often than not, it will become

a self-fulfilling example. Daughters and sons need to see Daddy treats Mommy as someone special. That tells daughters that they are worthy of respect.[16]

When our children were very small, I started intentionally opening the car door for my wife every time we got in the car. I had always opened doors for her, but not usually her car door. Frankly, it seemed a little courtly or old-fashioned. You don't see many men who do that anymore. But I wanted to model for my son how he should treat a woman, and I wanted my daughter to see how she should expect to be treated by a man. I also wanted to model honoring and cherishing my wife to them. Today, my son automatically opens doors for women without even thinking about it, and my daughter expects males to open doors for her and to treat her with respect. It was funny to watch in high school as she would stop at a door and expect the boys to open it for her. Of course, never having been raised that way, most of them did not know what she was doing. She would wait until finally one of them stumbled into opening the door and she would walk through and say thank you to him. You could see the momentary confusion on his face until the lightbulb went on as he understood what had just happened.

Another thing that is important is for you to garner respect for your wife. It is vitally important (even if you are divorced) that you make your children respect their mother. As our children were growing up I was quick to defend my wife's honor and make sure that they spoke respectfully to her. I would tell them, "That's my wife—don't speak to her that way."

Because a girl bases the value of a woman on what is modeled by her mother and on the respect her father extends to his wife, she needs to respect her mother. Respect is like a blackberry vine—when it gets a strong foothold, it grows no matter what you do. Your respect for your wife causes her to respect you. That respect is passed to your daughter, which is then passed on to her children. Give your daughter the gift of respect and love for her mother.

FOR DISCUSSION AND REFLECTION

- In what ways does a father have influence in his daughter's life?

- What effect do your words and actions play in the way she looks at herself and other men?

- Were you aware of those influences prior to reading this chapter?

- How will you use the power God has given you to be intentional in impacting your daughter's life? Remember—you *will* impact it significantly, whether you want to or not.

- Ask other men about examples of the influence they have had in their daughters' lives.

3

Communicating with the Female Species

See, women need to talk because they feel like they have to have adequate levels of communication in order to sustain a healthy and open relationship, whereas men are only driven to speak because of matters beyond their control, like not being able to find clean socks.

—Danny McCrossan

From sixth through eighth grade my daughter attended a small private school. Even though she played on that school's varsity basketball team, it was clear she was talented enough that she needed much steeper competition, especially to prepare to play high school ball. So she tried out for the larger public middle school team and made their varsity squad as starting point guard. That required me to take her to practice at the public school very early in the morning and then pick her up a couple hours later and take her to class at the private school. Since I was self-employed, I also picked her up after school most of the time. It was a bit of an inconvenience, but that time together quickly became "our" time. Even into high school I continued to take her to school and often picked her up afterward. I learned to use that time as an opportunity to communicate with her.

My communication style during these driving sessions consisted mostly of just listening (of course, during the early morning drives I might not have been awake enough to talk). Unless she asked my opinion by direct question, most of the time I just listened to what she had to say. I would frequently say "Huh" or "Really?" to one of her comments in order to keep the conversation going, but other than that I kept my trap shut. Or I would occasionally prompt her by asking how she felt about something or why she felt that way, but again, I mostly just listened. These times became a very important part of our relationship. Especially during high school when she was prone to pull away from me, this time together kept us connected. I learned quickly to read between the lines of what she was saying.

Words Have Meaning

Have you ever noticed that words are important to females? When I speak at father-daughter events, by far the most notes I get are from girls who are desperate for their dads to talk with them, to share with them their experiences and what they believe is important. Frankly, the girls (even at a young age) are frustrated that they cannot seem to break through this impenetrable, soundproof wall their fathers have around them. Over time, as they get older, I sense these girls closing down, perhaps realizing that they will never get the verbal nourishment they need from their dads. Because words are so important to your daughter, it is painful when you do not fulfill this fundamental need she has for intimacy with her father.

Verbal communication is as fundamental to nourishing a female as food is to a male. Your daughter needs to hear certain words from you—often—in order to assimilate them. Females process information and emotions through verbal communication. They also develop intimacy through conversation. For instance, your daughter needs to hear the words "I love you" frequently from you in order to assimilate that belief. I know as men we think our actions should speak louder than our words. Why should we have to say something that is so obvious? But females need to *hear* words in order to believe them as true. In fact, oftentimes you will notice that women have a tendency to believe a man's words over his actions. Many women will believe a man when he says "I love you" or "I want to marry you"—even if his demonstrated actions are diametrically opposed to those words. If a woman does not internalize feelings of love and worth about herself while growing up, she will often seek to fulfill that craving elsewhere. It's why many women are vulnerable to a man who knows how to speak a woman's language—to tell her all the things she needs to hear—despite his character.

There may be other reasons why females are more susceptible to men's words than their actions. The filter system women use to judge men is influenced by their fathers. Most of us know that women and girls are frequently attracted to "bad boys" or the wrong type of guy. Especially if their father abandoned or abused them, girls are almost irresistibly drawn to bad guys. Dr. Leman explains:

> It's my belief that these young women confuse abandonment and love because that's how their dads "loved" them. They want to believe their dads cared for them, even if their fathers were distant. This has radically distorted their filters. They don't expect loyalty; they don't see that trust is a vital part of a relationship. As long as they *feel* like they're in love, or as long as a boy *tells* a girl he loves her, she is convinced the love is genuine.[1]

This is why it is important for fathers to talk with their daughters. Not only does a father have the capability to speak emotional health and well-being to his daughter, he also gives her guidance in other areas of life. Besides modeling healthy masculinity, a father gives his daughter a male's perspective on life. Even more, she needs to believe she is valuable enough for her father to spend time with her. After all, the opposite of love is not hate—it is indifference. If we are indifferent about something, we usually do not believe it is worth spending our time on.

One very successful woman told me, "I wish men would realize how much their girls need verbal affirmation—because no matter what I did, it was never good enough. This has carried over into my marriage . . . the feeling like I'm never 'enough' no matter how much I do." Perhaps the deepest need of each human being is to feel appreciated. Our entire lives we ask ourselves questions such as, "Does anyone love me?" "Am I special?" "Am I appreciated?" Too many children grow up without getting good answers to those questions.

Your words have power with your children. They will remember things you said for their entire lives. Their whole life can be changed merely by something you say to them. Remember to use positive words in your everyday conversations with your daughter. People always respond better to positive feedback than negative, and your daughter is no exception. She needs her father's words of affirmation spoken into her heart.

While a mother might seem to be the natural one to fulfill this requirement for verbal communication, a father's words are very powerful. Here's what one woman said about her father:

> I wish he would have told me he loved me every single day. I wish he would have told me not to drink, not to experiment, and not to look for acceptance from my peers, especially the opposite sex. I wish he would have told me not to have sex before I got married. I wish he would have talked to me about setting goals and meeting

expectations. I wish he would have helped me make better decisions. I wish he would have just talked to me.

Perhaps because words mean so much to females, they are really affected by being lied to. Most females have an almost pathological response to being lied to. It seems to wound them even deeper than actions do. Remember that and recognize that even casual remarks or comments are interpreted by females as promises. When those "promises" are broken, it is tantamount to being lied to in a female's mind. That form of betrayal is seldom forgotten soon.

During childhood, mothers and daughters have a special, unique bond. They have a secret world that fathers are not a part of. As a girl gets older, her relationship with her mother changes from a primary caretaker to that of a friend. But beginning around adolescence, that close bond between mother and daughter often changes from "friend to rival, confidant to opponent."[2]

Oftentimes, especially during adolescence, the tension between moms and daughters can be strained and even stretched until it snaps. They frequently argue in a way that to a man can seem hysterical, if not brutal toward each other. I can remember confrontations between my wife and teenage daughter where words were flying, screams were escalating, and emotions were palpable. Moms take a girl's behavior (and words) personally. This is where a father's presence can become very important in the dynamic of the entire family.

Men and especially fathers can provide a more balanced, logical, solution-oriented approach when emotions get strained. Several times I had to physically intervene between my wife and daughter, pulling them apart and sending them to neutral corners of the home. Once I even stood between them with my hands on each of their foreheads, separating them as things got too heated. But being the logical, pragmatic voice of reason when emotions get carried too far means getting involved in emotional and uncomfortable (for us) situations. That requires us to use rational, controlled, and steady behavior in all circumstances. We'll discuss this further in the chapter "What a Girl Needs from a Father."

Understanding Her Language

Communication is a very important, yet often difficult, task between two independent individuals and genders who each have differing experiences, values, and perceptions. Females in general have more highly developed communication skills than males. Girls develop the right side of the brain faster than boys. This leads to early talking, larger vocabulary, better pronunciation, earlier reading, and better memory. Females also hear better, see better, have a better sense of smell and touch, and are able to read emotions on a person's face more easily than males. This gives a female, even at a young age, a big advantage with interpersonal communication skills because she can pick up on nonverbal cues much more readily than a male.

The corpus callosum is a bundle of nerves that connects the left and right hemispheres of the brain. A female has a larger corpus callosum than a male. This allows the two hemispheres of her brain to function better together and communicate back and forth more easily than a male's. MRI and other brain scanning studies have shown that during verbal communication both hemispheres of a woman's brain often light up at the same time. When she stops talking, usually one hemisphere or the other will stay lit, indicating brain wave activity. Conversely, when a man speaks, typically only one side or the other of his brain will light up. When he stops talking, both sides generally go blank.[3] Females can talk, feel, and think all at the same time. Males generally can't. Again, this is a result of men not being designed to be able to use the two hemispheres of the brain simultaneously as proficiently as women.

Females generally have a much larger vocabulary than males at all stages of life, and they typically use about two to three times as many words each day as the average male. In fact, as amazing as this is to me, girls and women like to talk—they actually enjoy it! They talk to process information and feelings. They talk with each other to be closer and more intimate. They like to talk to each other about their problems. What males don't realize is that when females talk to them, they are simply trying to establish intimacy. When a woman talks to a man, she is inviting him to share himself with her. When your daughter shares her concerns with you, she is not necessarily looking for you to provide a solution but just to listen so she can process the problem. This makes her feel closer to you.

Speaking Her Language

Part of communicating effectively with your daughter is to understand how to speak her language. Because words have meaning to females, they tend to place great emphasis on what is said to them and remember those words for a long time.

A female's thinking process is fueled by emotions and feelings, hence she tends to think emotionally rather than in a linear fashion like males do. We think of things in a logical progression (if we do this and this, then this will be the result—$a + b = c$), but women think of many different, and often unrelated, topics all at the same time. We men compartmentalize our thoughts and emotions, but women think on many levels and unconnected topics all at the same time. The billions of synaptic connections between the neurons in a typical woman's brain all appear to connect with each other in a frenzy of information overload (at least from the perspective of a linear-thinking being).

Have you ever been talking to your wife (or daughter) and suddenly realize you have no idea what she's talking about because it is a completely different subject than you were just discussing? I often wonder how the two (or three, or six) different subjects

52

my wife is talking about could possibly be interrelated. When she explains the process that connects them, I am often astounded at the complexity involved. The mere mention of someone's name can send her thought process off in a completely different direction than the topic at hand.

How to Listen So She'll Talk

Perhaps the best way to speak a female's language is to listen to her. Women tell me that the thing that makes them feel most important is when men they care about give them their full, undivided attention. It serves to make a woman feel important and valued. Since most men value their time above all else, giving our time to our daughters speaks to them of how much importance we place upon them in our lives. To this day I struggle with being distracted by work, cell phone, television, or things happening in the background when I should be listening to the women I love. You can feel the pain in this woman's statement: "I wish my dad would have taken the time to hear me and know what my dreams and desires were." To be ignored is a great insult. Your indifference says to your daughter, *You do not matter enough to warrant my attention.* When we choose to ignore our daughters by being distracted, we are sending the message that they are less important than everything else in our lives.

Females also want to discuss a problem until it is resolved. That is a trait that most men are uncomfortable with. Most of us men would rather do anything to avoid a conflict or disagreement in our homes. We like our "castle" to be an oasis of tranquility and quiet. We consider conflicts messy and even frightening. But females derive great peace and security when lingering problems and issues are put to rest. It's part of the way they are wired. Their need for relationship security and family well-being requires that problems be resolved as quickly as possible. That way they do not sit and fester until they become infected, rotting and destroying the relationship.

It is important for you to do several things so your daughter will understand that you are listening and that you care about what she is saying. First of all, as difficult as it may be, make eye contact with her while you are talking. That doesn't mean staring at her in an intimidating manner, but just that you make frequent eye contact with her so she knows you are engaged with what is being said. This will also require you to ignore the obligatory eye rolling that frequently occurs whenever you speak to her.

Second, listen at least twice as much as you talk (that shouldn't be difficult for most men). Then repeat back to her in your own words what you think she is saying. Do this frequently so you can be sure to understand what she is saying and where the conversation is heading. That ensures that you truly understand her and are not just thinking about changing the oil in the car. A young woman who is a friend of our son said, "Fathers need to actually listen and not just lecture their daughters."

Third, do not offer solutions unless she asks. That may be the hardest part of communicating with your daughter. Men are wired to fix things. We feel more comfortable doing things rather than talking about them. But remember your daughter processes information by discussing it. She is frequently just working through an issue when she talks about it so that she can figure out what she wants to do. Many times I've had to bite my lower lip until it bleeds to keep from offering unsolicited advice. But I've also noticed that when my daughter talks about a problem and I do not try and fix it, she often leaves by saying, "Thanks for your help, Dad—you're really smart."

Finally, be open and willing to address conflicts in your relationship. Do not ignore them, hoping they will go away—they won't. They just get worse and become more difficult to resolve. It confirms your love to your daughter when you do not allow problems in your relationship to persist.

Writing to Her Heart

Writing is a very effective form of communication. Some people even grasp more information by *seeing* the message than they do by hearing it. Even if daughters are too young to read, they treasure notes and cards from Daddy. Taking time out of your schedule to write to her shows your daughter that you are thinking about her even when she is not around. This is a yearning all females have—to be thought about in absentia.

I found letter writing to be a successful way to communicate with my daughter, especially when it was difficult to say things to her. Even short notes are very effective. Why do you think girls are always passing notes back and forth to one another? Well, I guess they used to—now they just text each other. But you get the point. In fact, if you are much more technically savvy than I am, you might text her during the day just to let her know you are thinking about her. Text her a short quote of advice every day. She might think it's corny, but I bet she'll look forward to your message every day.

Teenage girls are also really good at listening to a *portion* of what you say and then rolling their eyes and shutting down, ignoring the rest of your message. A letter requires the reader to "listen" to everything you have to say without interrupting. It also takes out all the subtle nonverbal cues (facial expressions, voice inflections, and so forth) that might skew

Tips for Writing to Your Daughter

- Write letters to each other—especially during times when communication is difficult.
- Be open and honest—it's often easier to write feelings than to say them.
- Put a handwritten note in her lunch bag or backpack before school.
- Send her cards in the mail (even if she still lives with you) for her birthday or other special dates. Take the time to write something from your heart. Remember that females actually *believe* the words printed on greeting cards.
- Give her a handwritten invitation the next time you take her somewhere special.
- Write down a list of all the things you like about her. Put a ribbon around it and give it to her for no reason.

the content of your message. I found that when hormones were coursing through my daughter's body, she just looked for excuses to argue or get upset. I could inadvertently distract her from the point of my message merely by the nuances in my voice or an unintentional "look" during a discussion. This, of course, allowed her the luxury of getting upset and stomping off instead of hearing my side of the issue. This is also a battle strategy that girls use in the war on parents. If they can get the emotional upper hand, they win the argument. It is also a form of control they can use to get what they want, or at least bend the discussion in the direction they want. By changing the discussion to an emotional plane, they garner control over it. Your challenge is to keep things logical and on task. Trust me on this—you are doomed to lose the upper hand if it devolves to an emotional debate.

But people cannot help but read what is written to them. The next time you get a card in the mail or someone hands you a note, try your best not to read it. You'll be surprised at how difficult it is—your curiosity always gets the best of your willpower! My daughter has kept nearly every letter I wrote her and has told me she still reads them frequently.

One woman told me, "My dad has written me three letters over the course of my life (one in college and two in my adult life). I treasure those letters to this day. I think dads have a harder time communicating verbally than girls."

Letters allow men to convey information (especially heartfelt emotional messages) that they might be intimidated to share otherwise. I can tell my daughter I am sorry and ask for her forgiveness

Letters from Kelsey (age 9)

My Father
Father, you are as loving as a father should be.
You work as hard as you should.
You provide a roof over my head.
You protect me as if you were a shield.
You are as kind as the most kindest father in the world.
You are as sweet as the most sweetest smelling flower I have ever smelled.
I love you as much as I can say.
From your daughter's heart,
Kelsey

much easier on paper than I can eye to eye. The words seem to get stuck in my mouth when I try to say them out loud (one of my many character flaws).

Letters or notes also allow your daughter to communicate with you on topics she may not be comfortable saying in person. Or if she feels you are not listening to her, she can purge those feelings of frustration by writing them down (that's why many girls keep a diary). I have several letters and cards that my kids gave me over the years. I keep the special ones in the inside cover of my Bible. I also have a couple of special drawings that Kelsey made when she was little that I have framed and hung on the wall of my office. Interestingly, they all say, "I love my sweet daddy." Whenever I feel down I just look at those innocent stick-figure drawings with hearts all over them, and I feel better.

Even as I am writing this, I picked up a legal pad from my desk to make some notes and discovered Kelsey had secretly written "Love you, Daddy!!" on one of the pages deep within the pad. Either she loves her dad or she's trying her best to look good while I am writing this book.

While verbal parlance is the best form of communication with your daughter, writing allows a man an additional form of interaction to supplement his attempts to connect with her. I found it to be very effective and helpful in the relationship with my daughter.

Whatever form of communication you use (and I encourage you to use multiple forms), it is important that you continue to try and communicate with your daughter. Start at an early age and persevere even when times are difficult. Good communication always results in better relationships.

FOR DISCUSSION AND REFLECTION

- Words, especially her father's words, speak directly to a girl's heart. Remember, she needs to hear words of affirmation daily in order to internalize them. Your words offset much of the garbage the world yells at her every day. Write your daughter a letter telling her all the things you love about her. If you are so inclined, text her messages each day telling her you love her. Develop a strategy with other dads to be intentional about speaking to your daughters each day.

4

Bonding with Girls

He is the hero of her childhood and often a wall she pushes against during her adolescence. He is often both the rule-maker, laying out laws of discipline and competence, and the rule-breaker, helping his daughter take risks, push the envelope, and explore uncharted worlds.

—Michael Gurian, *The Wonder of Girls*

I have a great photograph of my daughter when she was just a little girl having a tea party with my dad. The pictures show my tall, very reserved, and dignified father sitting in a tiny chair at a tiny table, sipping a fake cup of tea and wearing a woman's straw bonnet on his head with a feather boa around his neck.

Even the most hardened of men are putty in the hands of a little girl. After all, what father hasn't sat still while his daughter(s) put curlers in his hair, or conformed to all her make-believe rules while playing dolls with her? My hairline receded early in life from carrying my little girl around on my shoulders at places like the zoo while she used my hair for handholds, yanking it out by the roots.

When our daughters first learn to cook, dads are the ones who eat all their creations, no matter the taste, and rave about how good they are. The first meal I remember Kelsey cooking was supposedly some sort of alfredo dish, except the noodles were crunchy and stuck together. It also tasted like Elmer's glue. But I asked for seconds and told her I loved it.

Most girls have their daddies wrapped around their little fingers even as babies. I remember nuzzling my daughter and smelling that wonderful baby smell—there's no smell on the face of the earth like it. It smells like pure innocence.

As Kelsey got a little older I would brush and blow-dry her hair after her bath while we sang "Bingo" at the top of our lungs, the lyrics echoing around the tiny bathroom. Then I would read to her after tucking her into bed, all warm and snuggly in her flannel pajamas, smelling like apple pie and sunshine.

And then when she drove away in the car by herself for the first time, she took a piece of her daddy's heart with her.

That sweet little thing can get us to do almost anything for her, whether it be playing tea party, putting curlers in our hair, or spending our life savings on her wedding. All we want to do is protect her and keep her happy and safe from the world. But to do that we have to have a close relationship with her—and a close relationship means that we have to bond closely to her.

The following are important attributes to consider when bonding with our daughters.

Time

When our daughters are young we naturally bond with them, but as they get older it requires some intentionality. When they are little we can play with them by giving them "airplane" rides and horsey-back rides, but as they grow up these playtime gestures do not suffice or are inappropriate. Bonding with our daughters requires us to spend time with them—time doing what *they* want, not necessarily what *we* want to do. It might mean taking them shopping at the mall or going to lunch with them once a week. There are the special times as well; for example, I have pictures lined up on my dresser of me and Kelsey that were taken at the five Girl Scout father-daughter dances we attended.

Whatever we do, our daughters consider time spent with them as a demonstration of our love. While as men we often equate the amount of time we work or the material items we bestow upon those we care about with proof of our love, females in general aren't all that impressed with material goods. Trust me, all the fatherless girls we work with could care less about whatever gifts their absent fathers give them—they just want time with them.

Here's one woman's cherished memory: "Dad took me riding on his motorcycle. I have a memory from when I was about six or seven years old, hanging out with him at a mechanic's shop for most of the day. It was hot and sticky, and my dad shared a Coke with me. It was in the old-fashioned bottle and came from one of those machines that dispensed only bottles. Man, it was the best thing I'd ever had!" She didn't care about where she was or what she was doing. She didn't care that she was hanging out all day in a sweltering, dirty, greasy mechanic's shop. She was with her daddy. Just sharing a Coke with her dad was what she remembers after all these years.

My daughter was sitting around with several teammates after high school soccer practice one day. She was complaining about the fact that, even though I paid for her clothes, I always went along to make sure the clothes she bought were appropriate. None of the girls said anything for several seconds, until one of them sadly commented, "I'd give anything just to have my dad go shopping with me." Another girl nodded her head in agreement. That comment changed my daughter's attitude regarding her clothing purchases. This illustrates the importance our daughters place on our presence in their lives and our willingness to give them our most valuable asset—our time.

For dads who do not live with their daughters, giving them the time they need can be a challenge. I have been fortunate to never have experienced the heartache of the breakup of my family. I do understand though how many difficult situations this scenario presents. But I want to strongly encourage you to continue to spend as much time as possible with your children. Here are one woman's feelings: "Once my dad got remarried to a woman with two little girls, I felt like a distant cousin. I was not invited into their family very often, mainly at holidays. Please encourage dads in stepfamilies to include your bio kids in everything . . . or at least ask them!"

I understand that spending time with your children from a failed marriage can feel like facing a reminder of past pain and failure. I also understand that it can be frustrating and difficult to deal with ex-spouses. But while the pain children feel is devastating when they have to experience the destruction of their family, it is compounded even more with the loss of their father.

What All Girls Want

We have to learn to love our daughters differently than we love our sons, and certainly differently than we love our wives. We also need to recognize that each daughter is unique and needs to be loved uniquely to her personality. One of the ways girls feel loved is by our presence and our attention. Too many women I've talked to have vague or few memories of their father. He was gone from home too much or never attended any of their events.

Does your daughter feel valued in her home? Does she feel like she is important and loved? If not, she will seek value and acceptance elsewhere. Even more than money or material goods, she needs your attention and loving acceptance in order to feel good about who she is as a person. She craves your attention—it makes her feel valued. Her worth as a human being is validated when you acknowledge her unique qualities.

I love coaching basketball, which is interesting because it's the one sport I did not play in high school. When I first started, I coached recreation teams for several years before coaching the public middle school team for three years. Then for several years, I also coached the girls' JV basketball team at one of our local high schools. On away games I sat at the front of the bus while the girls sat in the back. If you've ever been around a dozen sixteen-year-old girls, then you understand—the noise can be deafening. One particular evening while returning home from a game, the bus was unusually quiet. As we entered town I heard a plaintive voice from the back exclaim, "There's where my daddy lives!" The sound of longing and sadness in her voice broke my heart. Suddenly several other voices piped up, "My daddy lives at such and such address. Where does your daddy live?"

Hearing these good girls long for their fathers was a humbling experience. I estimated from observations and from comments I'd overhead during the season that about half of the team came from single-parent homes. Remarkably, very few parents attended the games, and even fewer fathers ever showed up. Each of these girls was nice, well-mannered, and academically successful, yet each longed for the same thing—her daddy. I wish their fathers could have

Letters from Kelsey (age 11)

What a dad means to me. . . .

What my father means to me is a loving, caring, helpful dad that is strong and hopeful.

This poem belongs to a dad that does not beat me or touch me in a bad way.

A father is supportive of his family. A father is a man I can share my boy problems, but not just boy problems, but other ones.

My father is smart, sensitive, and so called "handsome."

A father is a person I love so much. And that father is you.

I love you so much dad. Happy Father's day, from Kelsey

been with me on that bus and heard the anguished cries of their daughters' souls into the night.

That's what your daughter wants—she wants her daddy.

Healthy Physical Affection

It is difficult to overstate the need a daughter has for healthy physical affection from her father. A girl who gets healthy physical affection from her father is not compelled to try and get it from any and every male who comes along and shows the slightest interest in her. She is not compelled to sacrifice sex in order to get nonsexual affection from the first male who shows her any attention. Meg Meeker says, "I've heard countless girls tell me they had sex with a boy (not even a boyfriend) simply for the physical contact, because their father never hugged them or showed them any affection."[1]

Girls who do get the affection they crave from their fathers go on to have a greater chance of leading healthy relationships throughout their lives. This woman tells how important her father's hugs were to her:

> I remember wanting my dad's hugs and having no problem getting them. He would take me out on the lawn mower with him when I was very young, snuggled close to him, or carry me in from the car when I had fallen asleep on a trip. But every night, I wanted Dad's good night hug and kiss, and I'd stay up late with a babysitter just to get it. Of course, time and adolescence challenges life and there were times when I didn't ask as often or he didn't offer so quickly, but even then, hugs were glue in our relationship. Now that I'm in my midthirties, I still look for my dad's hugs. And if I'm staying the weekend at my parents' house and he leaves the house without giving me one, I clear my throat and ask, "Hey, Dad, missing something?" and smile big. He knows just what I mean. I make sure that even now he knows some things never change—his hugs are always going to be special to his girl.

Adolescence is a time where great changes are taking place, both inside and outside of your daughter. This change can be a confusing time to both father and daughter. When my daughter was little she used to climb up on my shoulders in public, cling to my leg while I was walking, and wrestle on the floor with me and her brother. In the evenings she would jump up on my lap, snuggle in, and watch television. (She used to get very frustrated, as this immediately caused me to fall asleep; but to a man who worked long hours like I did, this soft little "heater" was an irresistible source of great relaxation.)

But as our daughters get older, this kind of physical affection becomes impractical or unacceptable, and we must learn to relate and bond in other ways—usually by talking and listening, which most men tend to be weak at. And their protests notwithstanding, teenage girls still desire a loving relationship with their fathers. Youth and family experts Chap and Dee Clark say, "Throughout the early years of adolescence, every daughter is almost desperate to have a warm, close relationship with her father, but the struggle, the fighting, and the misunderstanding often cause her to deny what she craves."[2]

Your daughter needs your hugs and kisses from the time she is a baby until you are no longer on earth. During adolescence she may shy away from this physical affection, and dad may be intimidated by her newfound sexuality. Respect your daughter's wishes in this regard during puberty, but let her know you are available if she does want a hug or a kiss. My daughter was very resistant to any physical contact with me during her teenage years, but by eighteen or nineteen she seemed to snap out of it and now wants a hug and kiss every time I see her.

Your Approval

Because a female develops so much of her self-esteem and self-image through interpersonal relationships, the relationship she has with her father means a lot to her. She craves her father's approval. Many women go to great lengths their entire lives trying to get the approval and recognition they crave from their fathers. One woman stated it this way: "Eventually I ended up working for my dad at the restaurant he managed to get the approval and recognition I so desperately wanted from him."

A father's approval means that a girl is okay just the way she is. It allows her to disregard much of what the culture dictates should determine her self-worth (beauty, sexuality, and breast size) and allows her to develop a healthy self-esteem based on her inner qualities. This is much healthier for her and leads to a lifetime of fulfillment, self-confidence, and being comfortable with herself. Girls who have a father's approval seldom suffer from the toxic tension, paranoia, and insecurity that many women suffer from today. A father who approves of his daughter gives her permission to face the world with confidence.

If your daughter believes you approve of her, she will be more self-confident and have a higher self-esteem. She will not be concerned about what others think of her nor will she feel the need to prove herself.

Her Rock of Gibraltar

The Rock of Gibraltar is a huge chunk of limestone off the coast of Spain near the inlet of the Atlantic Ocean into the Mediterranean Sea. The Rock of Gibraltar has long supported castles and other fortifications designed to fend off enemy attacks. Despite numerous sieges, it seemed that no forces could destroy the Rock or its inhabitants. This history has inspired the saying "solid as the Rock of Gibraltar," which is used to describe a person or situation that cannot be overcome and does not fail.[3]

A father needs to be a Rock of Gibraltar in his daughter's life. She needs his calm, solid presence in her life as the whirlwind of hormones and emotions thrash her countenance up and down like an out-of-control elevator. He needs to be there during the struggles, the troubles, and the attacks. He needs to withstand the sieges of adolescent rebellion and fend off the attacks of a culture that would use her up and spit her out for its own self-serving gratification. He needs to be her invincible rock, steady and able to weather any storm—no matter how difficult.

In the movie *Cinderella Man*, Russell Crowe portrays the true story of professional boxer Jim J. Braddock. Braddock had some success as a light heavyweight in the late 1920s, but the Great Depression soon made fight purses scarce. Losing heart for the sport, he ends up in disgrace and is finally forced to quit boxing after breaking his hand multiple times. Unable to support his family through manual labor on the docks, he watches as everything he owns disappears. His family slowly starves and his children become sick due to the cold weather.

One day his son steals a salami from the local butcher shop. When Braddock finds out, he walks his son back to the store to return it. As they leave the butcher shop, his son comments that his friend had to go live with his uncle because his parents couldn't feed him anymore. Braddock says, "Things ain't easy. Just cause things ain't easy that don't give you an excuse to steal what ain't yours. We don't steal—not ever." After eliciting a promise that he will never steal again, Braddock tells him, "And I promise you we'll never send you away." His son cries in relief.

During the cold winter, with the heat and electricity shut off, the children become sick. In desperation his wife farms the kids off to relatives who can feed and take care of them. When Braddock comes home to find his children gone, he says, "I promised him. I promised him with all my heart I would never send him away. I can't break my promise."

Braddock, in perhaps what was the ultimate insult to a man at that time, goes on public assistance. He then humbles himself in front of his former boxing peers and begs for a handout to get enough money to have the electricity turned back on and get his kids back home. He does what he has to do, no matter how hard, in order to provide for his children.

One day, due to a last-minute cancellation, Braddock's longtime manager gives him one more shot in the ring. Out of shape and rusty, he miraculously wins the fight against a top heavyweight contender. Invigorated and healthy again, Braddock suddenly goes on a winning streak against other top fighters. Out of a sense of pride, he uses a portion of his prize money to pay back money the government had given to him while he was unemployed. When his rags-to-riches story gets out, the sportswriter Damon Runyon dubs him "The Cinderella Man," and before long Braddock comes to represent the hopes and aspirations of the American public coping with the Depression.

Braddock eventually fights heavyweight champion Max Baer. Baer, a vicious and powerful fighter, is a ten-to-one favorite after having reportedly killed two men in the ring. On June 13, 1935, inspired by the love for his family, an old and arthritic James J. Braddock wins the heavyweight championship of the world. He eventually lost the championship belt to Joe Louis two years later, but Louis said he was "the most courageous man I ever fought." Braddock then served honorably in World War II, owned a construction company, and with the winnings from his championship fight, bought a home that his family lived in the rest of their life.

James J. Braddock was a gentleman throughout his life, even in the most trying of circumstances. But most of all he was a rock for his wife, two sons, and little girl.

The Damage of Our Wrath

My children and even my wife get shaken up when I get really angry, especially if I am loud about it. As men, we are used to and pretty comfortable with our anger. We learn early in life to use it for a variety of purposes—everything from giving us power and strength to helping us deal with physical and emotional pain. For many men, anger is a constant companion and even a frequent friend. But we don't realize how much it affects our children.

Females are a lot more tenderhearted than males are. Women and girls are more gentle and caring about people and their feelings. They tend to be more unconditional in their love while men are more performance-based in theirs. They are generally more accepting of others and their faults than men are. Females of all ages are more apt to fall for a sob story or try and rescue someone who claims to have been mistreated. They are more attuned to their emotions than men are and more sensitive to the nuances and shifts in relationships.

Because girls and women have bigger hearts than men do, they are more easily broken. I think Peter referred to a woman as the "weaker" vessel not as an insult to her mental or physiological strength, but in recognition of her more fragile and tender heart (1 Peter 3:7 NKJV). For this reason, a man's anger can be destructive to his daughter. His condemning, critical, and impatient spirit can wound her for a lifetime. His anger can easily break her tender heart. Many daughters carry around their father's harsh words their entire life.

Here's one daughter's advice to dads:

> Dad, speak positive words to her. When she needs correction, find ways to say what needs to be said without character assassination. The best corrections present better alternatives. This will build her self-confidence and capacity to think outside of just the emotional situation. Sometimes, the dad will need to discuss with the mom how to present corrections; Mom's perspective can balance things.

Don't shout or use profanity. To a daughter this means her dad is out of control. A daughter needs her dad to be her stable, safe place. She needs her dad to be the most wise, calm, intelligent, reliable, responsible, righteous person there ever was (and all the other qualities that describe God's character, too, since a father is his daughter's first example to lead her to God). Yes, that task is difficult. I know as well as any man my own failures in these areas. But half the battle is in the effort. You will fail and make mistakes, but keep trying—it's important!

Remember also, words matter more to females than they do to males. Females remember things that have been said to them and think more deeply about those words than we do. Think carefully about the words you use with your daughter. Your words can be tremendously healing or devastatingly wounding. A father who uses patient and gentle words with his daughter fills her with soul-healing nourishment to carry into the world. Used correctly, a father's words can help him bond with his daughter deeply, creating a lifelong relationship.

Create Lifelong Memories

I owned a white-on-black 1972 Chevy Custom 10 half-ton pickup truck from 1988 (the year my daughter was born) until I finally, albeit reluctantly, sold it in 2005. It was in excellent condition when I purchased it, and I kept it in good shape through all the years. We used it infrequently, as the big old 350-cubic-inch, eight-cylinder engine only got about eight miles to a gallon of gas. We used it for standard household chores, moving stuff, and hunting and camping. But one thing that we used it for every year was to go cut down a Christmas tree. We would pile the whole family in the cab, drive into the woods, pick out a tree, and chop it down. Later that evening we would gather extended family and friends, stuff everyone in the camper shell in back, and drive around looking at Christmas lights. Both of my kids remember those times and still talk about them every year. Even our distant nieces and sister-in-law, who only went once or twice, still fondly remember those outings.

Here's what Kelsey said about that truck: "I remember your Chevy truck. I LOVED that truck—everything about it—the smell—everything. I remember we used to take our dog Dakota to get washed—or when we all went to go get a Christmas tree every year (although we always fought over which tree to get). I remember you sometimes would let me steer, I really enjoyed that."

Be intentional about creating memories that your daughter can cherish. She will need memories to hang onto during the difficult times of life. After you are gone all she will have is memories. What kind of memories do you want her to carry of you and pass on to your grandchildren after you leave this life?

FOR DISCUSSION AND REFLECTION

• What is the most valuable and important gift we can give our daughters? (Hint: It starts with the letter "T.")

• Why is healthy physical affection from her father so important in a girl's life?

• Have you ever found yourself unintentionally hurting your daughter's feelings with your words? What did that look like?

5

What a Girl Needs from Her Father

Never, never, never, never give up.

—Winston Churchill

Winston Churchill was a man who knew a thing or two about persevering in the face of adversity. Churchill was a Nobel Prize winner in literature and was a noted statesman and orator. He served as Great Britain's prime minister from 1940 to 1945 and again from 1951 to 1955. He is widely regarded as one of the great wartime leaders, despite having suffered several political and military setbacks in his life. In the face of overwhelming odds, Churchill was the one man who refused to quit when most of his fellow countrymen were ready to throw in the towel against Nazi Germany. Consequently, he nearly single-handedly saved his country from defeat. Even though he previously had a speech impediment (which he worked hard to overcome), his speeches were of great inspiration to the British people during World War II. His countenance matched his physical appearance—that of a stubborn, determined English bulldog.

Churchill also suffered from severe bouts of manic depression (now known as bipolar disorder). The "black dog" was Churchill's name for his depression, and he appeared to struggle often throughout his life whenever the black dog would appear. But he did not allow this malady to curtail his greatness, nor to stop him from attaining his goals and living up to his responsibilities. Neither the loss of a child, poor health, or political betrayal kept him from serving his country with honor in its time of need. He did not quit.

Your daughter needs a dad who will not quit on her. She needs a dad who will not quit even when she is drinking alcohol, taking drugs, starving herself, or cutting on her skin with a razor blade. She needs a dad who doesn't leave when his marriage is on the rocks or when he loses his job. She needs a dad who continues to fight to provide for his family. She needs a dad who will persevere no matter what. She needs a dad who is a hero.

On April 3, 2010, David Anderson and his family were sightseeing in New York Harbor when a splash and a terrifying scream broke the calm. His two-year-old daughter, Bridgette, had fallen twenty feet off a historic boat docked at the South Street Seaport into the frigid East River. In what was described by witnesses as a "scene from a movie," Anderson raced down the deck of the ship and dove into the river to rescue his submerged little girl. As he rose to the surface, he lifted his sandy-haired daughter into the air and rested her faceup on his chest. Bridgette lay motionless for several seconds before she finally started crying. Anderson swam on his back to the pier where onlookers had lowered a rope, lifting both of them to dry ground. Both father and daughter walked away safe and sound with a story to tell their grandchildren.[1]

73

Girls need the following intangibles from their fathers. Be aware of these needs and focus on discovering ways to fulfill them in your daughter's life even from an early age.

Practicing Consistency

Perhaps the most important principle a girl needs her father to practice is consistency. Her world, especially during adolescence, will be one of mercurial ups and downs. She needs her dad's steady guidance and calm, objective presence. She needs a father who is balanced: strict but kind, loving, and forgiving. She needs a rock that she can depend on when all else is falling down around her.

Consistency is important when raising all children but especially with girls. Daughters thrive on knowing they can depend on their fathers to always be there for them. When she is little this might mean pushing her on the swings or tucking her in at night. But as she gets older she needs your consistent presence and level demeanor.

Oftentimes the little rituals that a father creates with his daughters are fondly remembered for a lifetime. Listen to the joy in these women's hearts:

Cheryl said, "I received a heart-shaped box of See's chocolates in the mail today—from my dad! He has given or sent me the same heart-shaped box of See's candy, with a hand-signed card, every single Valentine's Day since I was a little girl. Through many years and circumstances, it has always arrived on time. My dad . . . my hero."

Becky added, "Every year my father calls on my birthday and tells me the exact same story: 'We lost our first baby girl at birth as you know, so when I walked in and saw you in a little yellow dress on the hospital bed two years later, we could not believe how cute you were and that we'd actually get to take you home.' I told him it would not be the same without his call and my 'yellow dress' birthday story."

These women have benefited their entire lives from the simple attribute of their father's being consistent in his love for them. They know they can depend upon him and are buoyed by it. That confidence in their father's love gives them not only joy but also strength and confidence to face the world.

Giving Unconditional Love

Maybe more than anything else, a daughter needs her father's unconditional love. Love covers a multitude of sins and mistakes. I asked a good friend of mine how her father influenced her regarding dating and boys. She told me she never really had a very strong desire to date all that much. She said, "I was celebrated as a child and showered with unconditional love by my father. Consequently, I wasn't hungry for male love because I had it growing up."

During one of Kelsey's more rebellious "adventure" stages, she was driving our family minivan around town with her friends one evening. Apparently she honked her horn at a man and it provoked a road rage reaction in him. When they stopped at an activated railroad-crossing gate, the man (who had been chasing them for miles) got out of his car and smashed the side window of the van with a crowbar. Here was her memory of that event:

> There was the time I had to tell you about the van's window . . . THAT was one of the scariest things I ever had to do. Wake my dad up in the middle of the night and tell him that he's going to have to spend a lot of money to fix something that wasn't mine and that as a family we depended on. Man, I was shaking and on the verge of tears just from that thought alone! Forget the fact that I seriously thought I was going to DIE that night—literally! The thing I was worried most about was waking my dad up. But, to my surprise, you cared more about me than the van. You weren't upset; you just wanted to make sure I was okay, that I wasn't hurt. I think what daughters need to know is that their dads (even while it seems they

75

are more focused on material things) care more about them than they do whatever needs fixing. The fact that you didn't yell or get upset and asked me if I was okay meant more to me than anything in the world. And I think daughters need to know that their safety is more important than even a classic muscle car or a family van. In the end, dads don't care about those things, they love their daughters more.

While I appreciate Kelsey's sentiments, had she been in a classic muscle car instead of a minivan, my reaction might not have been as forgiving. Seriously though, our daughters do need to understand how much we love them. They need to know that we would literally give our lives for them if necessary. We express our love to them in two ways: telling them and then showing them by our actions. Yes, I was upset that she had been doing something she shouldn't have been and that our minivan was damaged. But I was more concerned that she was safe. She knew without me telling her or yelling at her in that situation that what she did was wrong (and dangerous). What she didn't know was whether her dad loved her more than the van. Now there is no doubt in her mind.

By the way, if you haven't already told your daughter that you love her so much you would be willing to die for her, I would encourage you to do so. That is an important thing to know, and you (and her mother) might be the only people in the world who would be willing to make that sacrifice for her.

Gaining Her Respect

One of the most important attributes a girl needs to have is respect for her father. It may even be more important that she respects him than that she loves him. That's not just because men require respect more than they do love but because it is healthy for *her* in all areas of life. Without that respect, she will founder in the rugged seas of adolescence.

First, your daughter will only follow your rules and abide by your boundaries if she respects you. When she is young she may follow them because she fears you and you are a natural authority figure, but as she gets older she learns that there is really nothing forcing her to follow your rules and guidelines. Our culture teaches her a disdain for authority, and she learns she is not bound by any laws to follow parental desires once she reaches a certain age. As a teenager she will only obey your rules for one of two reasons: because she loves you or because she respects you (hopefully both). If you try to force her through fear or intimidation, she will eventually rebel and you will lose influence in her life. But if your daughter respects you, she will willingly follow your wishes as she knows they are in her best interest.

One of the turning points in my relationship with Kelsey was when she was going through a difficult time at about sixteen years old. I took the time off work and spent the money to fly the two of us to Oklahoma City to attend a father-daughter summit sponsored by the National Center for Fathering. Not only did that time together on a special trip help us bond, but she also respected me for sacrificing the time and spending the money to invest in our relationship. She learned that I valued her and placed a premium on our relationship.

Letters from Kelsey (age 16)

Dear Daddy,

I know I never tell you that I love you. I know I should, but I don't quite work that way. I have my own way of saying that I love you, like the Snickers thing. That's one way I show you I love you. I really do love you though.

In the end I know I'll turn out good, and just know you totally helped me get that way. You've helped me so much over the years, even if you never said a word, just knowing you were my daddy was all I needed.

To be honest, everything I've said in this letter has nothing to do with what I am supposed to be writing about. But after today, I hope our relationship will be stronger and last forever. You're the greatest daddy a girl could have, I love you so much. Like you know I can write better than I can talk, but I'll talk when I'm ready.

Love ya always forever, Kelsey

PS—You are my hero, and my highest role model . . . and I so respect you for that.

77

Second, your daughter desperately needs your leadership. Your healthy, strong leadership will earn her respect. Pediatrician Meg Meeker says it like this:

> Whatever outward impression she gives, her life is centered on discovering what you like in her, and what you want from her. She knows you are smarter than she is. She gives you authority because she needs you to love and adore her. She can't feel good about herself until she knows that you feel good about her. So you need to use your authority carefully and wisely. Your daughter doesn't want to see you as an equal. She wants you to be her hero, someone who is wiser and steadier and stronger than she is.[2]

That requires you to earn her respect. You cannot be her hero if she does not respect you. You must be brave during times of trial. When she is pushing you and you want to avoid confrontation, you need to step up and enforce boundaries and earn her respect. If she learns she can manipulate you, push you around, or even intimidate you, she will suffer because of it. Make no mistake about it, a teenage girl's words, demeanor, and attitude can be intimidating to us men. Oftentimes we just want the conflict and drama to go away and leave us alone. But this serves no purpose except to give us some brief measure of peace and quiet. The storm will always return later with a vengeance and even more turbulence.

Here's how my daughter so eloquently expressed it: "Well, forcing me to go to church even when I didn't want to go helped me out. The fact that you didn't just pansy out and say 'okay, you don't have to go' the first time I put up a fight was a big help to me. I can't think of exactly *how* it was helpful right this second, but I know that it was."

We lose our daughters' respect when we fail to lead or fail to protect them. I have talked to many girls and women who have a burning contempt for their fathers. Almost always it boils down to the fact that their fathers did not enforce the rules and boundaries with them. A girl interprets that to mean her father does not love her, and she responds by losing respect for him—her only way of getting even for being rejected. Daughters (especially teens) *will* engage in power struggles with their fathers. It is their way of finding out if we really care about them. Ask yourself, *Isn't she worth the fight?* Your daughter needs you to fight for her. If you don't, she will look for someone who will—someone who may not have her best interests at heart.

Offering Encouragement

I've coached dozens, if not hundreds, of teenage girls in basketball over the years, and one thing I've learned is that despite their outward facade most of them are very insecure. They need to be encouraged and built up a lot in order to gain confidence. It is very easy to crush them with just a word if I am not careful. As a male coach (and potential substitute father figure), they take to heart everything I say. I've observed that with female coaches the girls do not seem to take things as personally as they do from me. Any criticism on my part toward them is magnified and taken literally.

A dad's encouragement can teach his daughter to value positive characteristics such as honesty, hard work, education, and independence. Mostly his encouragement teaches a girl her value. As the authority figure in the home and the most important first male in her life, your approval and encouragement can give her a positive self-image and self-esteem springboard from which to face the challenges of life.

One woman expressed the importance of a father's encouragement this way:

My very first thought to your question was "my dad believed in me." He believed in me even when I didn't have confidence in myself. His belief provided a foundation of support that I could lean on when I needed a boost. His belief gave me courage to take a risk—trying

79

out for the tennis team, going to college, going back to college as a single mom. He believed that I could be a good mom and that I was a good mom. He let me know that he was proud of me as a daughter, a woman, and a mother.

I miss my dad (just writing this makes me cry). I wish that he could be at my graduation from college with my bachelor's in nursing this December. I know he would say that he knew I could accomplish whatever I set my heart on.

A father plays a big role in how a girl feels about herself. His encouragement and approval help her develop confidence and a feeling of adequacy. While males usually compete and judge each other by performance, females often judge each other based upon physical beauty and the qualities of their relationships. A father who recognizes and comments upon his daughter's internal qualities, and not just her physical appearance, gives her a healthy self-image. When a father encourages his daughter's involvement in various activities, she has something that provides her with a source of self-esteem other than just her physical appearance, which she has little control over. Also, she is less likely to depend upon a male's sexual desire for her as the determining factor for her esteem and self-image.

A father can greatly encourage his daughter just by being involved in activities with her. The activity itself doesn't matter as much as the father's inviting her into it—working in the yard, building something, planting a garden, hiking in the woods, riding horses are all activities that can help her feel secure about who she is.

A variety of activities also builds self-esteem in young girls, depending on their personalities. Competing and succeeding in sports, academics, dance, art, music, drama, or auto mechanics are all activities that help girls find strength and self-image. My daughter took three years of auto mechanics in high school, and it was amazing how much it built her self-confidence. I'm not sure how much she actually learned during those three years—since she was the only girl in class, I noticed that the boys and even the teacher did most of her projects for her.

In fact, as your daughter starts driving, it is important to teach her basic automobile repair techniques, such as how to change a flat tire, how to check the oil, and how to safely jump the battery. That way she not only feels competent, but she is also not at the mercy of the kindness of strangers should she have a car problem. Also, that old trick that boys have used since the automobile was invented—car problems in the countryside—becomes a moot point when she can jump out and diagnose the problem.

Anything that allows a girl to feel that she can succeed is valuable and important. Most important is for a dad to show an interest in what his daughter is doing. This interest encourages her that

Advice from Women on How Dads Can Encourage Daughters

- Dads should spend time with them.
- Dads should tuck them in at night with a kiss and blessing, prayer, encouragement.
- Dads should read to them when they are young (and later with them).
- Dads should allow and encourage their daughters to "help" (be with you and hand you tools or whatever you can think up to include them) in what you are doing (e.g., yard work, fixing the car, taking out the trash). This builds relationship and the girl's value of herself.
- Dads should show their daughter how to do practical things like paying the bills, yard work, painting, basic car care, basic electrical stuff, goal setting (financial, personal, school, physical health, vocational). This builds courage, confidence, capacity to plan ahead, and the willingness to risk and sacrifice.
- Dads can ask little questions such as, "What was fun about today?" or "What did you do today?" or "What did you learn in school today?"
- Dads should stop and *look* at their daughters when they are asking these questions and *continue looking* at them as they answer.
- Dads should smile at their daughters.

she is worth your time. I've coached many girls' basketball teams where I never saw a good portion of the players' fathers the entire season—even at games. But when fathers are involved, their daughters are blessed. One woman joyfully said, "My dad taught me to love sports, to be a reader; to cook 'dad's dinners.' I have great memories of my dad doing everyday things with me that became special because he took the time to do them with me. One of my favorite dinners is still my dad's 'flour and brown' chicken. He cooked it at least once a week one autumn when my mom broke her ankle. He taught me how to cook it as well."

Time spent with your daughter being involved in her world also helps you know the challenges she faces. A dad who is sensitive to the struggles his daughter encounters is a shield against the cruelties of a hard world. One woman shared with me, "Dad knew that I wasn't really popular at school. I didn't date; in fact, I had never even been asked out on a date. He offered to take me to my senior ball. It was the nicest thing he ever did for me, and I have always cherished the fact that he wanted to do this."

The more fathers talk to their daughters and ask questions and interact with them, respecting their opinions or at least hearing them out, the stronger their girls will get emotionally. Fathers who encourage their daughters give them a huge step up in life. Without that encouragement, too many women go through life with feelings of worthlessness and despair.

Sharing Physical Activities

Males are generally more physical than females. Boys and men naturally process information and emotions better when we are physically active. We verbally communicate better when we are able to move around. We also reduce stress levels through physical activities.

Reportedly, about 60 percent of the US population is overweight, and since mentioning your daughter's weight or body shape is destructive to her self-esteem, a good way to help her stay mentally and physically healthy is to include her in your physical activities. Females place more emphasis than is healthy for them on their physical appearance. Additionally, eating disorders and negative body image are rampant among young women. One of the more effective ways researchers are finding to treat and even prevent eating disorders is to have daughters spend more time with their fathers.

There are many ways to be active with your daughter. Hunting and fishing are not just for sons, you know. Well, even though the number of women hunters is growing, my daughter was never too interested in tracking down and shooting Bambi with me. She did, however, enjoy fishing, hiking, camping, golfing, bicycling, going to the gym, and even shooting guns with me. The point was spending time together *doing* things. Since males bond best by doing things together, it only makes sense to use that technique with your daughter as well. And besides, your daughter will be more than excited about getting to spend time doing things with dad.

Physical activities are also healthy for her in other ways. Author and fathering expert Joe Kelly says it this way: "Physically active girls are less likely to get pregnant, drop out of school, or put up with abuse. The most physically active girls have fathers who are active with them!"[3]

Several summers ago, a couple of friends and I took our fifteen-year-old daughters wilderness camping together. We camped for four days alongside a stream just above the tree line on Broken Top in the Three Sisters area of the Cascade Mountains in central Oregon. None of the girls had been wilderness camping before, but they enjoyed themselves immensely despite having to haul their own backpacks up nine thousand feet of mountainside and spending four days with no toilet. We picked wild berries, slid down snow on the shaded pockets of glacier, and hiked with the dogs.

While the girls did make a mad dash for the indoor restroom at the first Dairy Queen we encountered on the way home, they appeared to be happy and content to have spent four days sleeping on the ground under the stars and eating freeze-dried food with their dads. I don't know who had more fun around the campfire at night—the girls hearing our tired old adventure stories for the first time, or us dads getting to tell them to a fresh audience. What I do know is that not one of those girls has ever forgotten that camping trip.

Speaking Truth

Girls need their fathers to speak truth into their lives. We live in a world where evil is considered good and good is considered evil. In our postmodern, relativistic world, there are no absolute truths. Your daughter will hear lies all the time. She will be told that she should seek out uncommitted, casual sexual relationships, that her body and physical looks are more important than who she is as a person, and that God does not exist. Words are manipulated to convince people to follow a specific agenda. Even the meaning of words has changed. Homosexuals are now "gays." Taggers are called "graffiti artists" when they are really vandals. Other legitimate words (e.g., niggardly, terrorist, black sheep, housewife) have been deemed politically incorrect and removed from our lexicon in an almost Orwellian Newspeak manner.

In her book *The Language Police*, Diane Ravitch documents just how easy it is to get a word, phrase, or idea banned from modern textbooks and references.[4] Ravitch asserts that textbook producers are beholden to small nonelected liberal educational boards in a few key states such as New York and California, and that few citizens know anything about these boards or who holds the seats of power. It's not difficult for an interest group to mobilize a campaign to bombard the educational board. Meanwhile, the public is not even aware that their words or values are under attack from this corrupt system.[5]

Commenting on the actions of anyone of color has become a hate crime. Even suggesting the discussion of topics such as abortion, affirmative action, or the *actions* of a person automatically makes you a racist or a hateful, judgmental, ignorant fool. Revisionism of history has also taken place in our educational system for a number of years. As George Orwell wrote, "And if all others accepted the lie which the Party imposed—if all records told the same tale—then the lie passed into history and became truth. 'Who controls the past,' ran the Party slogan, 'controls the future: who controls the present controls the past.' "[6]

Your daughter needs to hear from a man's (i.e., her father's) perspective what the great truths of life are. You cannot allow our culture to speak only its lies and falsehoods into her heart. If you tell her with conviction what you believe is true, she will believe that herself. Otherwise she is likely to believe what another man or authority figure tells her is true. She needs to hear her father's logical, clear-eyed, black-and-white opinion on issues of right and wrong—not clouded by female emotions, compassion, and well-intentioned ambiguity.

Here's an example that my brother-in-law shared with me:

> When I was a kid, I was with my dad and we ran into a group of Hare Krishna folks asking for money, handing out literature, and singing "Hare Krishna, hare, hare Rama." I told my dad they should make that illegal. He knelt down and looked me right in the eyes and said that would be a horrible day for this country, because that would mean we are not free. I asked him what he meant. He told me that if they take the free speech rights from the Hare Krishna, then somebody someday would make it illegal to be a Christian. That really shook me. So now every time I see Krishna or any other group in public saying or doing things I don't believe, I feel at peace and I'm a bit relieved because it means I still live in a free country. When I see a news report where someone is burning a US flag, I remember that people fought and died for their right to do it.

That father spoke truth into his child's life, and his son carried that message around inside him for the rest of his life. It was a lesson never forgotten. Had that father been wishy-washy or ambiguous, that lesson would never have taken hold. But a father's passion and convictions are never forgotten by their children.

Our culture will tell your daughter many lies. Advertisers want her to buy things she does not need, greedy corporations want her to believe lies about herself so they can sell her "cures," and various political and cultural ideologies want her to believe their worldview regardless of whether it is true or even healthy for her. Politicians and special interest groups make up outrageous statistics and promote them as the truth; the media quotes them without even confirming their validity.

In a fascinating book by journalist David Kupelian titled *How Evil Works*, there is a chapter that discusses the notion that nearly all politicians lie in order to manipulate the electorate. And they tell not just little lies; they knowingly tell big, outlandish lies. Kupelian writes,

> The power of lies is not so much in the little "white lies" that are part of the fabric of most of our lives. It's in the big lies. It's paradoxical, but we're more likely to believe big lies than small ones. How can this be? Wouldn't the big, outrageous lie be more easily discerned and resisted than the small, less consequential lie? You'd think so, but you'd be wrong. There's dark magic in boldly lying, in telling a "big lie"—repeatedly, with a straight face, and with confidence and authority.[7]

One of the greatest liars in history understood this principle completely. Adolf Hitler, in his autobiography *Mein Kampf*, said,

> In the big lie there is always a certain force of credibility; because the broad masses of a nation are always more easily corrupted in the deeper strata of their emotional nature than consciously or voluntarily . . . since they themselves often tell small lies in little

matters but would be ashamed to resort to large-scale falsehoods. It would never come into their heads to fabricate colossal untruths, and they would not believe that others could have the impudence to distort the truth so infamously. Even though the facts which prove this to be so may be brought clearly to their minds, they will still doubt and waver and will continue to think that there may be some other explanation.[8]

Our children need to be made aware that this worldview permeates our culture and that they will be pummeled by lies of all kinds. To offset that, your daughter needs to hear the truth. The validity of pure truth—biblical truth—needs to be presented clearly and concisely from a father to his daughter. She needs to know the truth that, despite what our culture tells her, premarital sex *is* harmful to her in the long run. That divorce is *not* the best way to fix a relationship. That truth itself is *not* relative, dependent upon one's own interpretation and experiences. There *is* absolute truth in the world—truth worth dying for—and your daughter needs to understand that. Otherwise she is doomed to be fooled and manipulated by people who have no interest in her except for how it can benefit them.

Of the hundreds of women I have surveyed over the years for my book research, one lesson from their fathers that stands out most in their minds is that of honesty. When a father was honest and taught the truth, it was absorbed into his daughter like moisture in a dry sponge.

Teach your daughter the absolute truth that she can be anything she wants in life, whether she chooses to be a veterinarian, a lawyer, a doctor, an astronaut, a writer, or maybe even president of the United States. Teach her to be free, strong, and independent. Teach her that there is nobility in fulfilling her roles as wife and mother if she so chooses. Teach her to depend on God for her self-worth, not on the opinions of a man or on her accomplishments in life. The truth is that the only thing holding women back today from being or doing anything they desire is themselves.

Being Transparent

Fathers who are transparent enough to admit when they make mistakes are a blessing to their children, especially their daughters. When a dad can confess that he has made a mistake or that he does not know something, it teaches his daughter to trust and respect him and, by extension, men in general.

One of the challenges many men face is admitting their weaknesses. Men, and fathers in particular, are often expected (or place the expectation upon themselves) to know everything. The truth is, our daughters know we are not perfect and, in fact, they do not expect us to be. But they do expect (or at least deserve) us to be responsible enough to admit our mistakes and ask for forgiveness. One woman said, "Dad, it is okay to come back to a situation and say you were wrong. This is the most humbling thing there is to do. What this teaches a girl is so deep in respect, value, honor, relationship building, acknowledging our humanity, and opens the door into God's plan for life and living."

Our model in this area influences our daughter's choice in men. If we only present this facade of being perfect, we can do great damage to our daughter's perception of men. Here's what one woman told me:

> My dad was such an amazing man, that I never saw he had any faults, and that ruined me. Every relationship and both my marriages were tough. As soon as I realized that the men I was with would never be like my dad (good, kind, pure, loving, totally perfect in my eyes), I would shut down. I had this standard in my head that no one could meet . . . ever. I thought if they could be just like my dad, then we could have it perfect. I so wanted a perfect man like him and each failed romance sent me searching for more. It wasn't until I was twenty-nine years old that my dad told me all of his faults, actually pointed them out, though I guess they were obvious all along. He wanted me to get over what I felt toward him in the sense of thinking he was so perfect. And once he started stating

his obvious faults, well, I started to see them. And it changed the way I looked at my own man—and myself.

I often find it is my stupid, stubborn pride that keeps me from being the husband and father I want to be. My pigheaded ego keeps me from apologizing, even when I know I should and sometimes even when I want to. I have to fight the urge of trying to present myself as perfect and never being wrong.

I can remember past bosses at work or superior officers in the service who thought they knew everything and never admitted they were wrong. If you've ever served under those types of men, you probably felt as disgusted and disrespectful toward them as I did. We shouldn't expect our children to feel any differently about us when we behave that shamefully. Frankly, I don't want my daughter to end up marrying some blowhard know-it-all just because I modeled that behavior for her. I want her to marry a guy who is honest, forthright, and brave enough to admit when he is wrong. That's the kind of man I want loving my daughter and raising my grandchildren.

FOR DISCUSSION AND REFLECTION

- Why is it so important that a daughter respect her father? In what ways do we earn her respect?

- Fathers give their daughters a great gift by speaking truth into their lives. What are some fundamental truths you think are important for your daughter to know? Make a list and develop ways to speak those truths into your daughter's heart on a consistent basis.

6

"Danger, Will Robinson!"

> Abandon hope all ye who enter here.
>
> —Dante, Divine Comedy
> (inscription at the entrance to Hell)

The world is a dangerous place for girls. Your daughter faces many physical, psychological, and emotional dangers. These dangers can cause a variety of behaviors that are harmful to your daughter. Eating disorders, poor body image, cutting, and depression are all symptoms of low self-esteem and/or emotional trauma in young women.

Especially during adolescence, a girl's self-esteem tends to drop. While she may badly want to be a grown-up at this stage in life, I recommend helping her stay a girl for as long as possible. Unfortunately, with all the depravity the world throws at our children, many parents feel compelled to grow their children up fast in order to protect them.

But girls raised in relative innocence and with constant primary attachments, who are protected and kept safe, end up being stronger, more competent, and less neurotic as adults than those who have been forced to mature early.[1] This doesn't mean that we shelter them or be overprotective, just that we provide intelligent, commonsense boundaries and guidelines for our daughters.

The following are some dangers that dads need to watch out for with their daughters.

Not Allowing Her to Fail

Perhaps the biggest mistake my wife and I made while raising our children was not allowing them to fail enough. We rescued them too often instead of letting them learn from the consequences of their actions and choices. This kept them from learning many valuable lessons necessary to succeed in life. Many parents of our generation have made the same mistake. Too many parents hover over their children, just waiting to swoop in and rescue them at the slightest sign of discomfort.

Allowing your daughter to fail teaches her great life lessons. By allowing "consequence behavior" to occur instead of being confrontational, dad can teach many good lessons. For example, if you told her to put her lunch money in her pocket and she forgot, she learns that going hungry for the day is the consequence. The natural consequences of her actions or inactions teaches her truths about life. Keep these lessons on "low consequence" situations where only a small amount of suffering is required, and she will learn lessons for things that have bigger and more egregious consequences.

Another unhealthy expectation we have for our children is that they will not make mistakes. Everyone makes mistakes—it's how we learn. The other side to this trap though is that a father needs to make sure that his daughter does not place unrealistic expectations upon herself. Kevin Leman says, "One of the most important things a father can do for a daughter is give her the freedom to fail. Perfectionism devastates young women."[2]

Because of unhealthy worldly influences, young women often place unrealistic expectations upon themselves. If they are not perfect, they think they are total failures. If they gain a few pounds, they think they are fat; if they don't get straight As on their report card, they think they are dumb; if they get a pimple or blemish, they think they are ugly; if they do not get asked to the dance, they think they are unlovable. A teenage girl's world goes from one extreme to the other with little middle ground.

Dad offsets this false mind-speak by reflecting back to his daughter what she needs most—affirmation from a male who adores and loves her unconditionally and in spite of any real or perceived imperfections. Too many girls only see disappointment, judgment, and criticism when they look in their daddy's face.

Children who are never allowed to fail never learn anything. People learn best by trial and error, falling and getting back up and trying again and again until we achieve success. Our children learn this lesson best by our example. Too many parents (fathers especially) want to project a perfect image to their children. Especially if they are Christian parents, they want to only model a perfect example. But our kids learn great lessons from our failures.

My kids seem to think that I am capable of achieving anything I set my mind to, and I probably am. But they also need to know the cost that comes with that success. They need to know that despite my success as a writer, I had thirty-seven rejection letters before I published my first book. They need to know that even though I earned my master's degree in education, I unsuccessfully defended my thesis the first time I presented it. They need to know that despite having successfully owned a small business for sixteen years, a lawsuit caused by a small mistake on my part resulted in it being closed down.

You're not perfect and your daughter knows it. Help her learn from your experiences that failing is part of life. Those who are successful are those who learn from their failures and do not give up. Quitting is a very easily learned habit. People who quit when they fail at something never accomplish anything in life.

Poor Self-Image

Females in our culture are prone to judge their worth and value as a human being by their physical appearance. The image of what a female should look like has been warped by the media and a profit-driven culture that project unhealthy expectations on young girls. One of the ways to help your daughter develop a healthy self-image is to encourage her involvement in extracurricular events such as sports, band, theater, choir, or other activities. Achieving success in these pursuits gives girls a positive self-image. Success makes a girl feel good about herself. If your daughter never experiences success, she will be forced to judge herself by the world's standards (i.e., her appearance).

A father plays a fundamental role in how a girl perceives herself—her self-image. We lay the foundation for how our girls feel about themselves as women. A father who believes his daughter is beautiful inside and out helps her to have a healthy perspective on her appearance and self-image. Joe Kelly says,

> My daughter is likely to choose a life partner who acts like me and has my values. So, I treat her and those she loves with respect. Remember (1) growing girls need to eat often and healthy; (2) fad dieting doesn't work; and (3) she has her body for what it can do, not how it looks. Advertisers spend billions to convince my daughter she doesn't look "right." I won't buy into it.[3]

The desire to be beautiful speaks to every female's heart. If you really want to hurt a girl (or a woman), criticize or make fun of her appearance. Those are deep, lifelong wounds that scar a girl's heart. Men don't seem to have this problem. Just the opposite—we look in the mirror and even we aging, potbellied, balding guys think we still look pretty dashing.

Although I don't like television programs that use plastic surgery to change God's vision of how a woman was created, I do occasionally enjoy watching TLC's *What Not to Wear* with my daughter. Many of the women on the show are so downtrodden that they actually believe they are ugly. They often project hard shells to the world as a form of protection. Clearly they live lives of distress and despair. It warms my heart to see their transformation after professionals have chosen the most appealing clothes with properly applied makeup and hairstyling to accentuate their natural beauty. These women blossom like graceful, gorgeous flowers when they realize that they are, in fact, beautiful—every one of them! Their whole demeanor and personality change—they are full of joy. Perhaps it's because God created women so beautiful that this is where the Evil One chooses to attack. Satan's minions whisper in a woman's ear, "You are ugly. You will never be good enough. No man will find you attractive."

Never tease your daughter about her weight! A study found that girls who were teased about their weight by family members were twice as likely to be overweight as girls who weren't.[4] Another survey found that by age thirteen, 53 percent of American girls are unhappy with their bodies, and that by age seventeen, 78 percent are dissatisfied.[5] That is a huge number of women who are dissatisfied with their appearance at a very young age.

The Evil One seems to have a special hatred for females. One of his greatest weapons against girls and women seems to be words. He uses those words to attack their self-image. He first deceived Eve in the Garden of Eden by whispering lies in her ear. He continues to deceive women today by whispering in their ears lies that prey upon their most vulnerable areas—looks and worth. He tells a woman (or a girl) that she is fat, ugly, weak, unattractive, unlovable, old, unwanted, or unworthy. He then uses our culture to reinforce those lies through media messages that are guaranteed to ensure that she feels bad about her beauty, her body, and her value. Women are so powerfully affected by these psychological attacks that they can develop eating disorders and body image distortions. They may even learn to despise themselves and feel undeserving of love, so much so that some women feel like they deserve to be physically and emotionally abused.

Girls and women today are susceptible to these lies, believing words spoken either in flattery or in deceit. Because of their nurturing nature, women look hard for reasons to believe what men and boys tell them. They also look for the good aspects in a male's character, almost to a fault, overlooking bad traits by overemphasizing any good traits they can find.

It is important to teach your daughter to overcome these attacks on femininity and help her to recognize the inherent value of females. She needs to learn early that women are to be honored and cherished. She needs to recognize the importance females have to the family structure, to relationships, and to a man himself. She needs to understand women's equal status with men as human beings in God's creation.

Eating Disorders

One of the extreme consequences of our culture's obsession with physical appearance and weight has been the proliferation of eating disorders among young women. Bestselling author Thomas Perry incorporates this obsession within his novel *Pursuit*:

> They all thought they were fat, and even if they were thin, they harbored some suspicion that they were fat inside, and were just managing to hide the truth by being thin. Even then, they had to hear people tell them they weren't fat, so they'd know they hadn't been caught yet.[6]

Eating disorders among young women are nearly epidemic, and the dangers associated with them cannot be minimized. My friend has a beautiful, intelligent daughter who developed anorexia nervosa at about age sixteen. She slowly deteriorated physically until she weighed about eighty-eight pounds. I can't tell you how much my friend agonized over his daughter's condition. He spent days and nights on his knees praying for her. He spent thousands of dollars on counseling and hospital care. He felt helpless to do anything about this dreaded disease that was slowly sapping the

Factors That May Contribute to Eating Disorders[7]

Psychological Factors That Can Contribute to Eating Disorders:

- Low self-esteem
- Feelings of inadequacy or lack of control in life
- Depression, anxiety, anger, or loneliness

Interpersonal Factors That Can Contribute to Eating Disorders:

- Troubled personal relationships
- Difficulty expressing emotions and feelings
- History of being teased or ridiculed based on size or weight
- History of physical or sexual abuse

Social Factors That Can Contribute to Eating Disorders:

- Cultural pressures that glorify "thinness" and place value on obtaining the "perfect body"
- Narrow definitions of beauty that include only women and men of specific body weights and shapes
- Cultural norms that value people on the basis of physical appearance and not inner qualities and strengths

Biological Factors That Can Contribute to Eating Disorders:

- Scientists are still researching possible biochemical or biological causes of eating disorders. In some individuals with eating disorders, certain chemicals in the brain that control hunger, appetite, and digestion have been found to be unbalanced. The exact meaning and implications of these imbalances remains under investigation.
- Eating disorders often run in families. Current research indicates that there are significant genetic contributions to eating disorders.

life from his treasured daughter. As she got worse, she was hospitalized several times and force-fed until she stabilized. After years of counseling and prayer, she appears to have this disease under control, but its presence still lurks in the background and is likely to be passed along genetically to her daughters.

It is estimated that currently 5 to 10 percent of American girls and women are anorexic.[8] Most young women go through periods where they are concerned over their weight. They also have many internal and external forces pushing them to obsess about eating and dieting. Most men don't understand these "demons" within their daughters. If you are like me, you're thinking, "Just eat and get over it—what's the big deal?" But the issue is much more complicated than that.

Eating disorders such as anorexia, bulimia, and binge eating are characterized by extreme emotions, attitudes, and behaviors surrounding weight and food issues. Eating disorders primarily affect young women, with about 90 percent of cases being diagnosed in females. Many celebrities suffer from eating disorders and have spoken out about their struggles, including singers Paula Abdul, Fiona Apple, and Victoria Beckham (Spice Girls); actress Kate Beckinsale; and *American Idol* winner Kelly Clarkson. Princess Diana also reportedly struggled with this issue during her short lifetime. Eating disorders can be deadly. Famous celebrities whose deaths have been attributed to eating disorders include singer Karen Carpenter, actress Margaux Hemingway, and Brazilian supermodel Ana Carolina Reston.[9]

The main categories of eating disorders include the following:

Anorexia nervosa is a serious, potentially life-threatening eating disorder characterized by self-starvation and excessive weight loss.

Bulimia nervosa is a serious, potentially life-threatening eating disorder characterized by a cycle of bingeing and compensatory behaviors such as self-induced vomiting designed to undo or compensate for the effects of binge eating.

Binge eating disorder is a type of eating disorder not otherwise specified and is characterized by recurrent binge eating without the regular use of compensatory measures to counter the binge eating.[10]

The exact causes of eating disorders are unknown but may include a combination of body-image issues, peer pressure, cultural pressure, genetics, as well as psychological and biological factors. Eating disorders are complex and poorly understood but are very dangerous and can be difficult to treat.

How you and your wife model body image is very important. If you put pressure on your daughter to look a certain way, or if you criticize the way other people look, it can send unhealthy messages to your daughter. It is also important for fathers (and parents in general) to model a healthy lifestyle, such as eating healthy foods, regular exercise, and good sleeping habits. Emphasize health and fitness over diet and thinness. Do plenty of outdoor activities as a family—bike rides, swimming, hiking, and walking the dog together are all activities you can initiate. This not only sets a healthy model, it also bonds you together as a family.

Additionally, monitor the things that influence your daughter. Television, movies, and magazines portray unrealistic examples of what girls should look like. Dr. Susie Orbach discovered that spending just three minutes looking at fashion magazines lowers the self-esteem of 80 percent of women.[11] Control the things your daughter sees in the media that may be unhealthy for her. You do have control of what she is exposed to, especially when she is younger, although it may be a difficult task as she grows up. Talk to her a lot (even at a young age) about the examples she is being exposed to in the media. Ask open-ended questions as you discuss these issues. For example, when you see rail-thin celebrities on TV, ask her thought-provoking questions like, "I wonder how much time she spends worrying about her weight," or "I wonder why the media portrays such unrealistic images of girls as the norm."[12]

Observe your daughter's words and actions regarding her body. Does she have healthy eating habits? Does she say she is overweight and is attempting to go on a diet? Again, do not be afraid to talk to your daughter about these issues, especially if you have concerns. Our natural propensity as males regarding these kinds of issues is to leave them to

Possible Symptoms and Complications of Eating Disorders[13]

- Acne
- Osteoporosis
- Polycystic ovary syndrome
- Cardiac arrest
- Scurvy
- Kidney failure
- Tooth loss
- Brain atrophy
- Death

our wives as being more qualified to talk about them. The truth is, though, many of our wives were brought up with the same unhealthy exposures and have an unrealistic perspective on healthy female appearance. As a father, you may have a more objective and perceptive view of potential problems in this area, since most men do not have as big a problem with body image as women. Most importantly, guys, do not ignore this issue. Too many fathers have regretted their lack of action in this area.

Cutting

Cutting is a form of self-harm where a person cuts their skin as a way to cope with the pain of strong emotions, intense pressure, or upsetting relationship problems. Reportedly, the act of cutting the skin until it bleeds releases endorphins that make the person feel better. Cutting is not a suicide attempt but is a coping strategy to alleviate emotional pain and trauma. Cutting is often performed with a razor blade or knife and is kept secret, usually done on the arms, legs, or torso—areas that are easily covered with clothing.

The problem is particularly common among young girls ages nine to fourteen.

In the novel *Suspect*, here's how one woman described the peace and calm she felt after cutting herself: "I had found something I could control. . . . I could decide how many times I cut, how deep I would go. I liked the pain. I craved the pain. I deserved it."[14]

Kids who self-harm often have other issues. They may have experienced other traumas in their life. Dr. Wendy Lader, clinical director for SAFE Alternatives, says, "They may have a history of sexual, physical, or verbal abuse. Many are sensitive, perfectionists, overachievers. The self-injury begins as a defense against what's going on in their family, in their lives. They have failed in one area of their lives, so this is a way to get control."[15]

For many kids, cutting is the result of a repressive home environment, where negative emotions are swept under the carpet, where feelings aren't discussed. It's a myth that this behavior is simply an attention-getter. Lader says, "There's a [painkiller] effect that these kids get from self-harm. When they are in emotional pain, they literally won't feel that pain as much when they do this to themselves."[16]

What to Watch For[17]

David Rosen, MD, provides clues that self-harm is occurring:
- Small, linear cuts. "The most typical cuts are very linear, straight lines, often parallel like railroad ties carved into forearm, the upper arm, sometimes the legs. Some people cut words into themselves. If they're having body image issues, they may cut the word 'fat.' If they're having trouble at school, it may be 'stupid,' 'loser,' 'failure,' or a big 'L.' Those are the things we see pretty regularly."
- Unexplained cuts and scratches, particularly when they appear regularly. "I wish I had a nickel for every time someone says, 'The cat did it,'" says Rosen.
- Mood changes like depression or anxiety, out-of-control behavior, changes in relationships, communication, and school performance. Kids who are unable to manage day-to-day stresses of life are vulnerable to cutting.

Some kids who self-injure are just regular kids going through the adolescent struggle for self-identity. They're experimenting. My daughter went through a short period of time where the group she hung around with was cutting (we learned this from her school counselor). While I have no proof, I suspect she also experimented with this in order to be part of the group. We had several difficult discussions about this issue in which she denied participating. But my wife and I remained vigilant about looking for signs of this behavior and continued to talk with her about it. The thing I remember most about the experience is my feeling of helplessness and abject fear. I could protect her from bad people, but how could I protect her from internal "demons" that might tempt her to harm herself?

"Between 13 percent and 23 percent of US teens have reported intentional self-injury,"[18] and within that number is a new form of extreme self-harm called "self-embedding." Self-embedding is where a person (typically an adolescent female) inserts objects made of glass, wood, metal, or other materials under their skin.

What should you do if you suspect your daughter is cutting? First of all, do not panic or become hysterical (and don't let your wife either). Talk to your daughter openly but calmly about this issue. If this is an ongoing problem and not just a form of peer experimentation, she may need immediate professional help. If not dealt with effectively, this issue can escalate and become serious and even life-threatening. Again, guys, don't wait and hope this issue will go away by itself. Even though it may be frightening, you must provide the leadership to help protect your daughter from this dangerous activity.

Friends

During adolescence peers become increasingly important in the lives of teenagers. To girls especially, relationships and friendships are an important part of their identity. Friends provide a huge influence on how teens think, act, feel, and behave. Sometimes that is good and sometimes it is not. Many young people from good families have been led down the path of destruction because of the negative influence of unhealthy friends in their lives. The entire time we raised our children, we had a sign on our family computer that read, "Show me your friends and I'll show you your future." That didn't seem to make much difference in the kinds of kids our children chose to hang around with, but the sentiment is very accurate.

Letters from Kelsey (age 15)

Me oh my am I glad you're my dad!

Daddy=
Adventure
Discipline
Dozens of
Your
Smiles

48 that's how old you are,
84 that's how old you're not.
You're my dad
And boy I am glad
I wouldn't trade you for a new one
And I am glad Frank's your son
He's a good bro, although . . .
You have all that dough
If I wasn't your daughter, I'd probably be a ho
You raised me right,
Tucked me in every night
You're my dad
And boy I am glad.

As parents—even of older teens—it is our responsibility to protect our children from unhealthy influences. Many parents think interfering with friendships is a violation of their children's "rights" as young adults. But we wouldn't hesitate to take action if our kids were hanging around with adults who were convicted pedophiles or known drug dealers. There's not much difference between those types of influences and the control that damaged or broken young people can have on our children's lives.

While a teen, our daughter always had a "rescuer" mentality in choosing friends. She generally picked the at-risk kids who didn't have either a mother or a father and tried to be a good influence in their lives. While her compassion and intent was admirable, it often placed her in situations and circumstances that, had she had less-involved parents, would have resulted in disaster.

It is important that we be actively involved in the social lives of our children. It is important to know their friends and even their friends' families. While we didn't particularly care for many of Kelsey's "at-risk" friends in high school, we always tried to have them over to our house as often as possible and to show them a model of acceptance. We invited them to attend church with us, to dinner, and on gatherings and outings. I also made it my business to meet their fathers (or my wife would meet their mothers). Frequently we did not allow Kelsey to spend extended periods of time at these girls' homes because they were, in our opinion, unhealthy or unsafe environments. But we would allow their friends to spend time at our home. We couldn't always dictate who her friends were, but we wanted to influence the ones she chose as much as possible.

Additionally, because of our greater life experience, we were often able to gently predict the behaviors and outcomes of her friends and relate it to how they were raised. Even though she frequently rejected our advice initially, this allowed Kelsey to see that we had wisdom in this area. She quickly learned to value our opinions.

Depression

Depression is a significant issue with young women today. Over 35 percent of all high school girls experience, for at least short periods of time, what many physicians would term clinical depression.[19] Stresses of adolescence, breakups with boyfriends, mean girls at school, and the hormonal ups and downs of puberty can often lead to feelings of depression in girls. During adolescence, increases in hormone levels and hormonal imbalances have a tendency to increase the level of depression in teenage girls. In particular, higher levels of progesterone and the sudden drop of estrogen during her monthly cycle tend to make her feel more down or even depressed.

Additionally, girls who are sexually active also have a higher incidence of depression. In fact, Meg Meeker considers depression in teenage girls an STD (sexually transmitted disease), because it is almost always linked to underage sex.[20]

In her book *Five Conversations You Must Have with Your Daughter*, Vicki Courtney cites a study by the National Longitudinal Survey of Adolescent Health, which found that 25.3 percent of sexually active girls ages fourteen to seventeen reported they felt depressed "a lot of the time" or "most of the time," as compared with 7.7 percent who were not sexually active.[21] Another study found that sexually active teenage girls were more than three times as likely to be depressed and nearly three times as likely to have had a suicide attempt than girls who were not sexually active.[22]

Even if your daughter is not sexually active, she has a greater propensity to suffer from depression than you or your son does. Long-term clinical depression is not something to trifle with. It is dangerous and should be treated like any other disease. Because this pitfall ran in my family, I always felt that I would rather be safe than sorry regarding this issue. We had no problem asking a counselor or a qualified medical professional to talk with our daughter whenever a cause for concern arose. I'm sure Kelsey felt sometimes like we were meddling in her affairs, but she also knew we loved her enough to be concerned about her mental health.

Spoiled Rotten

Our culture has evolved from one of working hard and earning what we want to one of self-focus and self-interest. People (including children) expect the best for nothing. Not only that, but we have become a people with no gratitude for what we have or what is given to us. Many of the people our ministry works with are not very grateful for the things we give them, such as free resource materials or low-cost admission to our seminars. In fact, we can depend on the fact that those who do not pay will be the least likely to show up, despite our going out of our way to make accommodations for child care. And if they do attend, they will be the most likely to complain and write lower evaluations than the people who paid.

Have you ever been around an ungrateful teenager? You know— the one who does not appreciate the fact that her parents have paid the mortgage every month, put food on the table, paid for braces, and provided every other conceivable need she's had for the past sixteen years or so. Our children today, perhaps more than any previous generation, have an entitlement mentality. During the sixteen years I owned an environmental engineering firm, I interviewed and hired dozens of young people straight out of college. Nearly to a person they had unrealistic expectations of what they would be doing, how much they would be paid, and what benefits they would receive. Most seemed to feel that they should start out at the same pay and prestige level that their fathers had after working for twenty-five years. I was hugely disappointed at the lack of self-motivation and work ethic most of them displayed.

When I first started a full-time ministry, money was tight. Kelsey was about fifteen years old at that time. Being a good steward of the resources God provided every month required me to pay the bills in order of importance: mortgage first, followed by utilities, then all other bills. Last on the list was cable television. One month I did not have enough money to pay the cable bill, and our cable was shut off. Kelsey asked her mother why the television wouldn't work. My wife replied, "I guess your dad must not have paid the bill."

You'd have thought I had sentenced her to live in a Russian gulag. My wife finally said, "You have a job. Why don't you just pay the bill yourself?" After stammering and sputtering for several minutes, Kelsey finally replied, "No, because Frank will watch TV!" We laugh about that now, but at the time it was a clear indication of the entitlement mentality and ungrateful attitude that she had. In fact, if I recall correctly, my wife did not even have to point out her folly but merely looked at her, causing her to slink away in shame for having made such an obviously selfish comment.

I frequently see mothers and fathers who let their children run through the store screaming and yelling, totally unsupervised. This teaches children a number of negative lessons, including lack of respect for others, self-centeredness, and lack of self-control and self-discipline. They then scream for items at the checkout stand until the parents give in and buy something for them, if for no other reason than to just shut them up. Kids learn to use that method of embarrassing their parents to get what they want. If that happened when our kids were little, I would just calmly suggest that the offending child come out to the car and have a "talk" with dad. I only had to do that once or twice before the lesson stuck.

The need for instant self-gratification is ingrained in all of us. When this need is fed by parents who give little Johnny and Jenny everything they demand, it is like throwing gasoline on a fire. It explodes into a full-blown conflagration of self-focused behavior and creates the next type of problem—the narcissist.

Daddy's Little Princess

Some fathers give their daughters everything they could possibly want. Sometimes this type of behavior assuages a guilty conscience for not spending enough time with their daughter. Other times it fulfills a need within the father (an older man) to have a daughter (a young woman) fawn over him in a dependent manner.

Don't overindulge your daughter, creating a princess who expects everyone to serve her and the world to revolve around her whims. Doing this creates a narcissist. A narcissist is someone who is in love with and is fascinated with herself. Narcissism is characterized by an inflated sense of self-importance, need for admiration, extreme self-involvement, and lack of empathy for others. Narcissists also believe they're superior to others.

While only a small percentage of the general population is diagnosed as narcissists, a growing number of young people are exhibiting higher levels of narcissistic tendencies. In data from 37,000 college students, narcissistic personality trait scores rose faster in the 2000s than in previous decades, with the shift especially pronounced for women. By 2006, one out of four college students agreed with the majority of items on a standard measure of narcissistic traits. And nearly one out of ten Americans in their twenties has experienced symptoms of Narcissistic Personality Disorder (NPD).[23]

Today with social network sites like Twitter and Facebook, you can literally reach millions (if not billions) of people with the click of a button on your computer. Self-made celebrities like Lady Gaga have made millions of dollars and become overnight sensations by using Twitter to reach adoring fans. The ubiquitous presence of cell phone cameras allows you to upload personal movies and record real-time events on video websites like YouTube, which can then go "viral" and be watched by millions of people within minutes. You don't need to go to film school today to be a famous movie director or producer.

Nearly everyone today yearns to be an instant celebrity, and their fifteen minutes of fame is seemingly easier and closer than ever. But there is little distinction between fame and infamy anymore. TV shows like *The Jerry Springer Show* and *The Steve Wilkos Show*, where people allow themselves to be humiliated beyond the bounds of human decency (or good taste) in order to get a brief taste of fame, affirmed the notion that "any press is good press."

Teachers and parents are so focused on praising children in an attempt to create a false sense of self-esteem that they are creating egotistical little monsters. Just watch television shows like *Bridezilla* or MTV's *My Super Sweet 16* if you doubt that. This feeling of narcissistic entitlement allows children to feel justified in manipulating others to satisfy their own desires. Celebrities are bad enough, but the average American seems to have developed a monumental egotism as well. I am always stunned by the self-centered and self-focused behavior of the average person—just drive down any road and you'll see multiple examples.

Recently my wife and I attended a concert at the local zoo. The concert was to start at 7:00 p.m., but most people arrived about five o'clock to reserve a space, putting their blankets and chairs on the grass to get the best view of the band. However, a number of people came breezing in at about 6:45 and had no compunction against moving people's chairs and squeezing into the spaces up front that they felt they deserved. I was taken aback by the gall and entitlement attitude of these people, but no one else seemed to mind or think it was unusual. Thankfully no one infringed upon my space, since I would not have shown as much grace and self-control as others did.

What has this pursuit of self-focused pleasure won us as a society? Skyrocketing divorce rates, abortion, a plague of sexually transmitted diseases, sexual abuse and trafficking, pornography addiction, broken families, and on and on. And the good life—what the Greeks called *eudaimonia* ("a life well lived")—is a foreign concept to most people today. At least the perception of what a life well lived means has changed dramatically. A life well lived used to mean serving others for the greater benefit of humankind—a simple life with traditional values. We now live in an age of entitlement, in which a life spent pursuing material goods and ego gratification is encouraged. Materialism can be especially alluring to females. Author Michael Gurian says, "Female biology and acculturation both enjoy the beauty of small objects and the increased status of material wealth."[24]

So how do you keep your daughter from being self-focused to the point of showing narcissistic tendencies? While your daughter needs legitimate praise, she also needs to understand that the universe does not revolve around her. If she is praised and given too much, she will become dependent upon the approval of others for her self-esteem. She will also become overly sensitive to the criticism of others. She needs to understand that while she has an inherent worth merely by being a child of God, she also has a responsibility to use her gifts to make the lives of those around her better.

Help your daughter understand that she is merely one small piece of the universe, not its center. Despite her accomplishments or the fame she may achieve, she will be, like all of us, forgotten in a very short period of time after she passes from this earth. The only exception to that rule is that her family and those people in whose lives she makes a difference will be the ones who remember her legacy.

FOR DISCUSSION AND REFLECTION

- The world is a dangerous place for girls. How can you strategically help your daughter have a healthy self-esteem and self-image?

- The other side of the coin is, how do you help your daughter from being a self-centered "princess" who thinks the world owes her everything?

- What will you do if your daughter does develop an eating disorder, or begins to exhibit signs of self-harm?

- Ask other fathers how they have dealt with these situations. Develop a plan for actively addressing these issues should they surface. Better to be educated and prepared and not need it, than to need it and not be prepared.

7

Protecting Her

I cannot think of any need in childhood as strong as the need for a
father's protection.

Sigmund Freud

In the movie *The General's Daughter*, a young woman is a cadet
at West Point. She is the top of her class, putting the male cadets
to shame by soundly trouncing them both academically and
during physical training exercises. In her sophomore year, she is
separated from her unit during a large-scale night training opera-
tion. Six men from another unit, who hate her for besting them,
beat her, stake her to the ground, and brutally gang-rape her the
entire night, nearly killing her. At dawn she is finally found by her
unit and rushed to the hospital. Her father, a general in the army,
is notified and rushes to the hospital. But along the way he stops
for a meeting with a higher ranking general and is convinced that it
would be in the best interest of the army, the country, the academy,
and his career if this whole "episode" were forgotten.

At the hospital the woman is overjoyed to see her powerful father who has the ability and connections to avenge this terrible crime against her. Surely he will be her hero and make sure justice is served. But to her disbelief and tragic sorrow, he tells her to just forget it ever happened. He crushes his daughter's soul by betraying her love and trust when she needs him most, all for the sake of his career and a misguided sense of patriotism.

I graduated from high school in the 1970s. Things seemed so much more innocent then than they do now. Today the world is a tough and frightening place, especially for young girls who are naive and innocent but think they're not. The world is full of ugly and dangerous stuff. Meg Meeker says, "Even though she may not participate in ugly stuff, it's all around her: sexual promiscuity, alcohol abuse, foul language, illegal drugs, and predatory boys and men who want only to take something from her."[1]

Your daughter needs a father who will protect her. Today many parents confuse protection with control. They think if they impose boundaries and rules in their child's life, they are somehow being controlling. But protecting and controlling are two separate concepts. Protection keeps your daughter safe; it prepares her to succeed in the world, it equips her to be honorable, and it gives her a healthy self-image. After all, if her daddy cares enough to protect her, she must be worth it. Control is just the opposite: instead of setting a child up for success, it sets them up for failure. Being overcontrolling will cause your daughter to rebel and will cause you to lose influence in her life.

With that in mind, let's look at some ways that fathers can and should protect their daughters.

Physically

In early 2002, in the small town of Oregon City, Oregon, twelve-year-old Ashley Pond disappeared on her way to school. Two months later her friend Miranda Gaddes also disappeared. Neither girl was ever seen alive again.

The main suspect in their disappearance was the father of a friend of theirs, a man named Ward Weaver III. Both girls had reportedly been sexually abused by Weaver. Weaver had a long history of alcoholism and sexual abuse toward women. Ashley had even previously accused Weaver of raping her, but authorities failed to follow through on her accusation. Eight months later Weaver was arrested for raping his son's nineteen-year-old girlfriend. His son immediately told police Weaver had confessed to murdering the girls, and police and the FBI finally got a warrant to search Weaver's property. They found one of the young girls buried under a concrete slab behind his house and the other in a bag in a storage shed on the property.

That story was horrible and the gruesome details were in the news for months afterward. But what was not in the news is the fact that Ward Weaver III's father, Ward Weaver Jr., is a serial killer on death row in California for murdering a young girl and burying her under a concrete slab behind his house. The senior Weaver is suspected of having murdered up to twenty-four people. He was called "pure evil" by one journalist who covered the case and likened him to Hannibal Lecter from the movie *The Silence of the Lambs*.[2]

Ward Weaver III followed directly in the footsteps left for him by his father. But even worse was that neither poor little Miranda Gaddes nor Ashley Pond had a daddy at home to protect them from someone like Weaver. Both girls were products of broken homes and both had absent, uninvolved fathers.

Apart from her being raped or killed, I can't imagine too many things more horrible than seeing one's daughter posing in a men's magazine, starring in a pornographic movie, or working as a stripper or prostitute. And yet when men do not fulfill their roles as protectors in their daughters' lives, this is the fate that awaits many young women.

Recently I read a chapter from the book *Silent War* by Henry J. Rogers. In this chapter the author interviews five women who have been victimized by the sex trade industry (pornography, stripping, prostitution, adult movies). Even though not all of the women, or even the author, recognized it, after reading their histories it was clear to me that every woman was in her current situation due to the actions or inactions of her father.

I know there are a lot of factors involved in domestic violence (sexual, physical, emotional, or psychological), but it seems to me that if men were more proactive in policing their own gender by protecting girls and women from this type of abuse, it would be a lot less common. To stand by knowing this is happening and not do something about it seems criminal and unmanly to me. To engage in this behavior is not only dishonorable, it is cowardly and despicable. *Make sure whether you live with your daughter or not that she has a safe home to live in.* It's part of your responsibility as a father to protect your daughter physically—no matter the circumstances.

I knew a man once who went through a horrible experience. During a camping vacation their seven-year-old daughter fell off a bridge into the raging stream below. He leaped in after her to save her. He managed to grab onto her a total of six times over the course of several miles while being carried downstream in the roiling water. But the water was so fast and so powerful that it ripped her from his hands each time he got ahold of her. They eventually found her tiny, drowned body several days later.

Although I was at a stage of my life where I did not cry very much, I wept unashamedly at the memorial service for the little girl. The father's recounting of his heartbreak and despair over not being able to save his little girl broke my heart. I think all fathers can relate to the frustration of not being able to physically save and protect those entrusted to our care.

Emotionally

One of the more powerful emotional and psychological attacks our daughters face today is in the form of bullying. I'm not sure why, but females seem to me to be brutal in their treatment of each other. Even the 2004 movie *Mean Girls*, based on the book *Queen Bees and Wannabes: Helping Your Daughter Survive Cliques, Gossip, Boyfriends, and Other Realities of Adolescence* by Rosalind Wiseman, documented the treacherous nature of teenage girls toward one another. Most girls and women are familiar with cliques and the damage they are capable of inflicting on school-aged girls.

One young woman told me about her traumatic experience:

> I remember being at school and having to go to the bathroom so bad. I was in the bathroom when a bunch of girls, the mean bully girls, came in and started climbing on the walls and looking over into the stall (to this day I don't like public bathrooms), and they started making fun of me and wouldn't go away so I ended up peeing my pants. I had the walk of shame after that and I thought my mom would be so mad at me for having peed my pants, and having to leave work to come and get me, but when the principal explained what had happened, my mom was more worried about me and mad at them.

Bullying in schools is becoming an increasingly bigger problem. The American Psychological Association estimates that a shocking 90 percent of fourth through eighth graders report being victims of some form of bullying. Kids are subject to several forms of bullying, including physical, verbal, or social. Bullying is not just physical abuse; it is not limited to punching, pushing, or hitting. The internet and social networks provide unrestrained opportunities for bullies to abuse their victims with no accountability. Girls especially seem to be susceptible to cyberbullying. Their more tender hearts and need for relationship and acceptance make them vulnerable to verbal and written attacks on their character. Author Paul Coughlin says, "Bullying is 80 percent verbal. Girls perpetrate most of it in the form of 'relational aggression'—saying mean things and spreading lies—leaving the target feeling ashamed, isolated and powerless."[3]

This cyberbullying, in the form of spreading rumors and lies about another through spoken or written words via electronic media, is perhaps more destructive than physical abuse. Kids fear that everyone at school will see them bullied all over cyberspace—for example, on Facebook or MySpace, or through instant messaging, text messaging, email, blogs, cell phones, or chat rooms. One girl told me there was a whole page on MySpace devoted just to hating her.

In their blog article titled "Very Mean Girls—Two Generations Look at Abusive Females," Deedra Hunter and Elizabeth Whittemore give us some insight into the psyche of today's young women:

> When a guy walks into a room, he doesn't think much about it. When a girl walks into a room, she knows every other female eye will be on her immediately judging. Girls always pit themselves against other girls, no matter if they be friend or foe. Girls these days are mean and bitter, and it's not something that happens overnight in high school, it starts as young as preschool. Just as quickly as they become friends, they turn on one another. Girls have made a game of making each other feel small. Gossip used to be spread by simply word of mouth, but then the internet came along and gave the game a whole new set of rules.[4]

The newspapers are full of incidents where teens have been bullied to the point of committing suicide (known as bullycide) in order to escape the abuse of both their peers and even adults. Paul Coughlin writes,

> One national poll revealed that at least a third of teens have had mean, threatening, or embarrassing statements made about them online. In Illinois alone, researchers estimate that a half million kids have been victimized by cyber-bullying. Ten percent were threatened with physical harm (which is a crime). There's even software that allows people to text and instant message people as if they are someone else. There is no conventional way of tracking down the impostor. The anonymity allows bullies to be even more malicious.[5]

Girls who suffer from bullying often become depressed, do worse in school, and even fake being sick to avoid going to school. As a father, stay attuned to your daughter's countenance. If she becomes despondent, find out why. Then take a proactive approach and work with school administrators to understand and stop the damage of bullying. Too many girls and young women have taken their own lives recently as a result of being bullied; fathers must not ignore this issue. To find out more information about bullying, you can go to websites such as www.theprotectors.org.

Mentally

Adolescence can be a very confusing time for girls. It is a time fraught with fears, illusions, and false assumptions. Most of the fears that girls have are actually mental inaccuracies or hypersensitized illusions. A father can help his daughter sort through the following issues using his highly developed logical and objective thought process.

I have come in contact with many women over the years through my ministry and the books I have written. Perhaps because the work we do touches soft spots in their hearts, these women have a tendency to share their wounds and fears. Understanding the fears females in our culture face has been an eye-opening experience. Even though men have many of these fears as well, they seem to be more intensified in females.

While your daughter quite likely has some of these fears already, she will almost certainly experience many of them as she gets older. A father who is aware of these fears and doubts can develop a strategy to prevent them or to help his daughter overcome them. Without this knowledge it is difficult for her to even know that she has any fears. She then will likely respond to circumstances through emotional programming instead of using a proactive, well-thought-out response.

Many women I have spoken with say that they struggle with a variety of fears. Adult women have fear of being an inadequate wife and mother, fear of not being considered beautiful, fear for their children, fear of being abandoned, fear of change, fear of loneliness, fear of failure, and fear of losing their man to another woman.

All females also have a strong fear of rejection. Especially for those who have experienced rejection in their lives—by their fathers, by other girls and women, or by their lovers—rejection nearly becomes an obsession. When girls like this become adults, they are easily rejected. They tend to place too much emphasis on their husband's (or any man's) opinion of them instead of on God's, giving their husband the power to emotionally reject them. Then when they feel slighted or rejected by their husband, their entire world falls apart, stifling them in a lot of areas of life. Their fear of being rejected paralyzes and even debilitates them.

Girls and women also fear not being considered beautiful or wanted by a man. They often derive their self-worth from whether a male chooses them to date, marry, or even mate with. A girl who is considered unattractive suffers not only her own self-doubt and recriminations but also taunting from her peers. To be "wanted" and pursued by a male is a key component to her self-image. Girls who do not get asked to dances or out on dates believe something is fundamentally "wrong" with them.

Additionally, many girls who want to be wanted by boys will go to great lengths to please them. In fact, one study of teenage girls published in the *Archives of Pediatrics and Adolescent Medicine* found that 41 percent of girls ages fourteen to seventeen reported having "unwanted sex," claiming they did so because "they feared the partner would get angry if denied sex."[6]

Your daughter will be faced with many struggles in life, but inaccurate or unrealistic mental fears shouldn't have to be one of them. Do not let her be afraid of things that may not ever happen or are not that important to begin with. Again, your perception of her is the one she will likely carry through life. Empower her to believe in herself by teaching her how special she is in your eyes and in God's eyes.

Economically

In ancient Rome, fathers (*pater familias*) were head of the family. Roman law and tradition established the power of the father within the community and his extended family. A man had a duty to father and raise healthy children as future citizens of Rome, to maintain the moral propriety and well-being of his household, to honor his clan and ancestral gods, and to dutifully participate—and if possible, serve—in Rome's political, religious, and social life. In effect, the *pater familias* was expected to be a good citizen.[7]

Fathers also had the right of *patria potestas* over their children. In other words, a daughter had to have the consent of her father before she could marry. One of the ways a father determined an appropriate suitor for his daughter was by requiring a dowry. While the father collected and often administrated the dowry, it belonged to the bride and was passed down to her children (generally sons) upon her death. The dowry fulfilled several requirements. First, it demonstrated sincerity on the part of the prospective groom. It also determined that the groom was financially solvent. Most importantly, it provided the bride with economic protection upon divorce or the death of her husband.[8]

My friend's future father-in-law turned him down three times when he asked to marry his daughter. He finally gave his blessing, but he had been concerned that my friend could not financially support his daughter. It is a tribute to the character of my friend that he honored his future father-in-law's wishes each time.

Your daughter needs your financial support. Especially if you and her mother are divorced, she needs your economic strength. Kids from single-mother homes are much more likely to live in poverty than kids who live with their fathers. Yes, I know that sometimes women use visitation rights to hurt the fathers of their children. That's difficult, but it doesn't excuse your obligation to provide for your child. A good and honorable man does the right thing for the right reason, in spite of the outcome. Whatever issues are between you and your ex-wife, your daughter (or son) is innocent. When fathers do not provide financially for their children, the children are the ones who suffer. When your children get older, they will know who has acted in their best interests and who has acted selfishly. Kids need to know their father always puts them first, even at his own sacrifice.

Sexually

One evening my daughter and I were in a local restaurant for dinner. By the age of fifteen, Kelsey had blossomed into a gorgeous young woman. As we walked across the restaurant, I observed three males watching us from across the room. It was obvious that they were a grandfather, a father, and a son—three generations of men standing in a row. All three males had the same drop-jawed, glazed look on their faces as they leered at my daughter the entire length of the restaurant. My first instinct was to go over and slap all three of them. But after gaining control of myself, I recognized that here was a perfect example of the generational influence of men—the lack of respect that an older man has for women, passed down throughout the generations of his lineage. Upon further consideration, I decided I just wanted to slap the grandfather.

Remember the movie *Taken*, starring Liam Neeson? In the movie Neeson plays a highly skilled former CIA agent whose seventeen-year-old daughter is abducted in Paris, France, by the Albanian mafia, who sell her into sexual slavery. Neeson swings into action, quickly tracking her down through the seedy underbelly of Paris. In his crusade to rescue his daughter, he leaves a trail of maimed or dead villains in his wake. It was a movie that spoke to every father's heart.

After watching this movie with my daughter, my wife stated, "If that ever happened to you, that's what your daddy would do." Without hesitation my daughter replied, "I know he would!"

Now, I don't have any illusions that I can fight as good in hand-to-hand combat as Liam Neeson did in that movie, but I certainly wouldn't hesitate to shoot as many bad guys as necessary to rescue my daughter from a circumstance like that. The fact that she knows her father treasures her enough to go to those lengths not only gives her a sense of value, satisfaction, and well-being, but it also makes me feel good that she understands my love and esteem of her.

One of the strongest duties of a father is to protect his daughter sexually. While this might be considered old-fashioned or even controlling by today's modern society, I don't know of many men who do not have this instinctive impulse. Some men go to great lengths to protect and defend their daughter's honor and virtue. Fight for your daughter's virtue—and don't apologize about it either. If you don't fight for it, no one else will. Too many segments of our culture are calling her to throw away her purity. She needs her father to stand firm on this issue.

For dads who are divorced and do not live with their daughters, this can present a difficult problem. Girls from single-parent homes are much more at risk for sexual abuse, especially if the mother lives a promiscuous lifestyle. Living in a situation where large numbers of biologically unrelated men are brought into the home can have a number of significant consequences for your daughter, none of which are very healthy for her. Daughters caught in such circumstances face a much higher occurrence of molestation. Research tells us that approximately one in four girls is sexually abused before their eighteenth birthday.[9] These statistics are based only on the cases that are reported, so it is possible that it happens with much more frequency, since it is estimated that up to 60 percent of sexual assaults are not reported.[10] In addition, such a situation also models the type of behavior your daughter is likely to emulate regarding dating and relationships.

The act of sexual assault on a girl is bad enough, but the long-term effects can be even worse depending upon several factors.

Sexual assault is especially devastating if the perpetrator is the victim's father, stepfather, or grandfather. These are men who are supposed to protect her from harm, not the ones who do the harming. How a girl's family responds also plays a factor. A family who does not believe her or accuses her of making it up causes great damage. This can cause the girl to question the reality of the act. Later in life she may be involved in an abusive situation but continue to stay in it because she does not believe it is that bad. Perpetrators of sexual violence also go to great lengths to ensure their victims' silence. They often threaten the life of the victim or tell her that no one will believe her. A common tactic is to threaten the life of the girl's mother or father.[11]

We talked to both of our children at a pretty early age (and frequently while growing up) about protecting themselves and "listening" to those feelings in their stomach. If someone wanted to do something that made them feel "funny" or bad in their stomach, they knew it probably wasn't right. I told my daughter right up front and often that if this ever happened to her not to worry about me being harmed—regardless of what she was told. The perpetrator was the one who better be worried about his health. Part of the problem is that children often feel like their parents are omniscient and know everything. So they often assume that their parents know about the abuse.

The healing process for sexual assault starts when the victim tells someone and is believed. A girl who has been abused faces a variety of feelings, including shock, anger, grief, sadness, depression, helplessness, powerlessness, guilt, and confusion. It is important that she work with a professional who can help her identify and process all her feelings. She also needs to know that it is okay to be angry at the abuse. Depression is often anger that is internalized. Girls and women have a greater tendency to internalize anger than males who have been abused, and so they suffer more frequently from depression.[12]

My good friend's sixteen-year-old-daughter was upset with him when he wouldn't let her date a "very nice" twenty-two-year-old man from church. She was even more upset when she found out later that the "nice" young man had recently been convicted of statutory rape for impregnating a fourteen-year-old girl. She was also very grateful that her dad had stuck to his convictions.

Girls who are sexually abused often have feelings of inadequacy that they struggle with their entire lives. One woman described her feelings this way:

> Although I first tasted love from my grandparents, their love could not protect me from the sexual abuse that was taking place in my home from eighteen months old to the age of sixteen or the physical abuse that happened on a daily basis. I learned very early in life that my worth, love, and acceptance was based on my performance. That belief moved me into the world of performing arts and modeling where my sense of worth was easily filled by a well-performed song, dance routine, well-acted play, or display of skill on the runway. The harder I worked, the more my identity was tied to what I did and covered the worthless feelings I felt.

Those feelings of worthlessness created a performance-based mentality. So many girls and women today have their self-worth tied into their looks, whether men are attracted to them, or how much they accomplish.

It is important for a girl's recovery that her father seek justice for any abuse she has suffered. So as not to promote anything illegal, I suggest going through the legal system for recourse in this situation. But a girl who is powerless against her attacker often recovers better when the wrong done her is satisfactorily avenged, especially by her father. A woman I know very well was raped by a man when she was only fourteen years old. She did not have a father to avenge her and has carried that wound for years. I told her if I ever saw him, I would take matters into my own hands to obtain justice. Even though she has put this episode of her life behind her, she uncontrollably wept tears of gratitude at my offer.

Another area where a woman's father plays a major role is in her actual sexual decision-making process. For instance, girls with uninvolved or absent fathers tend to become sexually active at an earlier age than their fathered peers. They also have more sexual partners.

Women who have not had a model of healthy masculinity in their lives often have trouble detecting predators, abusers, and men who will abandon them. They are in some ways like a lamb left to the wolves. Oftentimes, these women continue to choose the same type of men, getting the same results over and over again. We often see women continue to select men who either abandon or abuse them. We can't figure out why they choose those types of men. Perhaps that was the type of manhood that was modeled for them and they have no greater expectation for themselves or their relationships.

Relationships

When Kelsey was about sixteen years old, she surreptitiously got involved with chat lines on the internet. My wife had previously installed software on our home computer that allowed us to see what she was emailing to other people. My wife did not consider monitoring software a violation of our children's privacy, and upon further reflection on the subject, I believe she was right. She saw it as fulfilling her duty as a parent to protect her children. One day my wife came to me and said that Kelsey had met a man on the internet and was planning on meeting him. We questioned her about this man and she said he was twenty years old (which was too old to date her anyway) and that he was "a good guy." (Interestingly, she never asked how we knew about this guy.)

Since warning bells were clanging in our heads, we had a policeman friend of ours run a criminal background check on this guy using the name and phone number he had given our daughter.

Imagine our surprise (not!) when we discovered this guy was really a twenty-eight-year-old man in another state with a criminal record as a sex offender.

Here's the deal, guys—I had several choices in this situation. One, I could have forbidden her from seeing this loser, but how many of you think a sixteen-year-old girl would have responded positively to that ultimatum? Right, she probably would have snuck out the first chance she got and met him. Two, I could have threatened his life, but how do you think he would have reacted? He might have been frightened off, but he might have taken it as a challenge. Not a risk I wanted to take. So, here's what I did.

Our policeman friend told us that there was nothing they could do until he did something illegal (like rape or murder her, I guess). However, he suggested that most predators will run from girls who have a male protective presence in their lives because it is too much trouble to deal with. There was much easier prey in girls who did not have fathers in their lives. Armed with that knowledge, I gave our new "friend" a call one day. He did not answer his phone but called my number back right away. When I answered the phone, he very aggressively demanded, "Who is this?"

I calmly replied, "I am Kelsey's father, the girl you have been communicating with online for the past month or so, and I understand you are planning on meeting her." There was a pregnant pause on the other end.

"I just want you to know that I have run a criminal background check on you and know your name and where you live. I'd like to know what your intentions are regarding my daughter."

After stammering for a minute, he said, "Uh . . . we are just friends."

I said, "Well, then I'd also like to know what business a twenty-eight-year-old man has being *friends* with a sixteen-year-old girl— who is still a minor, by the way. It doesn't seem like a very wise decision for a grown man to make."

I think you get the drift of our conversation. Frankly, I was surprised he didn't just hang up on me.

In conclusion, Kelsey and this guy continued to communicate online with each other for a while, but it was clear that this man was not as eager to meet my daughter as he had been before. They never met, and today he is long gone.

Despite my initial inclinations, I was able to maintain my composure and even speak respectfully while talking with this guy, which I think stopped things from escalating. Remember, "A gentle answer turns away wrath, but a harsh word stirs up anger" (Prov. 15:1). I didn't even have to threaten to show up at his house with a baseball bat and a bunch of my buddies (many who have daughters had eagerly volunteered for a road trip). I have to admit though, it took some courage and a lot of self-control to make that phone call. I had to fight my inclination to be passive and force myself into action, but I also had to fight my instincts to charge in and protect her physically. But that courage protected my daughter from a potentially very dangerous situation.

What do you think might have happened to my daughter had I not intervened? The sad truth is many women in our country are damaged by the actions or inactions of their fathers. As men we need to make it our mission to protect all women and children, not just our own daughters. Too many women have grown up to be victimized by men whose only desire is to satisfy their own self-indulgent needs. It breaks my heart to learn that between 100,000 and 300,000 girls a year are kidnapped and sold into the sex trafficking industry here in America. Most of these are "throwaway" kids from foster homes or drug families. Many have been sexually abused from a young age. But some are daughters just like yours and mine who were in the wrong place at the wrong time. The average age of these girls is thirteen, with some as young as eight or nine years old. They are generally transported across several states and sold multiple times. Once captured and traumatized, it is nearly impossible for them to escape on their own. Imagine what it feels like to be in this situation and believe no one cares about you, except to use you as a commodity. Imagine what it feels like to have no one there to rescue you from evil.

Several young men who have recently dated my daughter have told me, "Don't worry, I can and will protect your daughter in a fight if I have to." Frankly, that attitude didn't exactly instill a high level of confidence in me. I had to explain to them that while that is important, there is more to protecting someone than just physical protection. Ensuring that you have the long-range vision to keep her away from situations where she might be exposed to physical violence is just as important as physical protection.

Young women are much more at risk in our culture than they believe they are. And despite the fact that they rail against our rules and restrictions, most daughters eventually recognize and appreciate their fathers' protection.

FOR DISCUSSION AND REFLECTION

- A father's very presence in his daughter's life protects her in many ways. In what ways does a father protect his daughter?

- What does that look like in your life?

- What if a father does not live with his daughter? How can he still provide protection for her?

8

The Truth about Boys

For some unknown reason, bad boys draw you in despite the fact that they are jerks.

Alexis Bledel

My friend Brad told me the story of when he wore a younger man's clothes. He lived in an apartment complex near his friend Tom. One day an older man came to his door looking for his friend. As he opened the door, the man said, "Excuse me, do you know where Tom lives?"

Being a young smart aleck, Brad answered, "No, but I know where you can find some wax for your bald head," and slammed the door in the man's face.

A year or so later Brad started dating Tom's cousin. The first time Brad went over to her parents' house to have dinner, the very first thing he saw was a picture of her father. Guess who? You're right, the bald-headed man! Frantically, Brad tried to convince himself that the man would not remember him; after all, he had joined the military in the intervening time and was slimmer, with shorter hair. Alas, her father eyed him carefully for the first part of the meal before slowly saying, "I know who you are."

Brad says he and his father-in-law have a good relationship today and laugh about that incident, but it was a pretty inauspicious start.

Even though I would have preferred that my daughter not date any boys until her midthirties (and you probably do too), the truth is your daughter *will* be dating (eventually anyway) and there's not a lot you can do about it. Rather than denying reality, it's best to prepare her in the best way possible: help her understand what boys are like and why they are like that. I always (somewhat) jokingly told my daughter that all boys were evil and that they traveled in packs like dogs, marking their territory and sniffing around girls. It was a familiar joke between us but also established a picture in her mind that we discussed over the years. She saw many situations and circumstances that matched my description pretty well.

What Boys Want

All men know what teenage boys are like. We were young men once. If sex isn't the first thing on their minds, it's not very far from the forefront. I know some fathers will argue that their sons are different and not obsessed with sex. In fact, I had a long (one-sided) discussion with a pastor I admire who denied that his sons fit that stereotype. Out of respect, I conceded that his sons probably were not like every other young man on the face of the planet. And I concede that maybe one in a thousand young men aren't either, but I think most of the men who feel that way about their sons are probably deluding themselves. The truth is young males are biologically predisposed to procreate and are at the height of their sexual prowess in their late teens. Young men who do not act on that are to be even more admired—not because they don't think about sex but because they have the self-control and discipline not to seek instant gratification.

Both male and female bodies contain testosterone, with males having much more than women. While prepubescent boys and girls have about the same amount of testosterone, during puberty the average boy's testosterone production increases tenfold or more.[1] This increase in testosterone causes strong and powerful urges for sexual release. Most young men are fairly creative in what they'll do to fulfill these urges.

I know I'm being hard on young men. Not all of them are as bad as I am portraying them. In fact, there are probably quite a few respectful, God-fearing young men out there who are dedicated to staying sexually pure until marriage. (I've just never met them personally—I've heard about them, but never met them.)

I can't imagine that many, if any, young men will entirely meet my approval for my daughter. The truth is, I myself certainly would not have met my standards for her when I was a young man. Frankly, I don't know what my wife saw in me, and if she had a father around, I'm sure he would have been concerned about me as well. Not that I was a bad guy, but I was a broken and angry young man with a very large chip on his shoulder.

Most young women are as attracted to boys as boys are to them. Unfortunately, males are also just as confusing to them as girls are to boys. Hence, dads provide a good source of information for daughters on how boys think and why they do what they do. For instance, we all know guys like food. Heck, I married my wife because (besides being incredibly hot looking) she could cook my garbage and make it taste good. There's a funny television commercial showing two young women in a club. One of them is carrying bacon in her purse in order to attract men. It quickly works—a crowd of men surround her and dreamily say that the smell is "intoxicating." My wife once heated up some pizza at work, and every guy who walked in the office the rest of the day commented on how good it smelled. Tell your daughter she doesn't need to spend money on expensive perfumes—just dabbing a little cold pizza behind her ears is all she needs to attract men of all ages.

Most young women want to know why boys act the way they do. Explain to your daughter that during adolescence, testosterone begins to course through a boy's veins, causing many changes. His voice drops, he develops muscle mass, he gains facial and body hair, and he can become more easily agitated. Testosterone also changes a boy's behavior, causing him to be more interested in attracting the attention of girls, primarily through actions such as engaging in risky behavior, competing with other males, and becoming more territorial. These behaviors seem to be cross-cultural and occur in all young males no matter their environment, heritage, or race. Testosterone levels explain many of a young man's behaviors.

You can also explain to your daughter that even though some boys might look like men, they generally are more emotionally immature than girls are. Tell her that boys don't particularly like to talk, and that just because he doesn't tell her she's beautiful doesn't mean he doesn't think she is. Additionally, boys are generally not as interested in deep, committed relationships as girls are.

What She Needs to See

It's important for your daughter to see what authentic masculinity looks like so she is not fooled when she sees a male who is not authentic. Your good model of how a man thinks, acts, solves problems, loves a family, and lives life is critical because she uses that as a yardstick to measure other men. This is important because it's easier to spot a fake after you've seen the real thing. That's how FBI agents learn to spot counterfeit money. They study authentic bills over and over again until they can easily spot a counterfeit bill when they see it.

One group your daughter needs to be aware of and protected from is older boys and/or high-risk boys. These types of males have the ability to exert a great deal of influence over girls and young women. When Kelsey and her friends went from attending a small private middle school to a large public high school, many older girls warned them about the propensity of older boys to prey upon naive incoming freshman girls. They warned them of the dangers of older boys manipulating them for sexual favors.

During my daily summer bike ride today, I approached two muscular young men on bikes. They were shirtless and all "tatted up." Riding right behind them was a well-developed young woman who was also bare-breasted. I know they probably thought this was a hoot, but it made me wonder if this young woman had been raised by a loving father or one who was absent or abusive. Being with young men who would allow or encourage her to act this way in public did not seem like the healthiest of choices or one that a girl with a loving father would have made.

Things Your Daughter Needs to Know about Boys

- Always be honest. Guys hate duplicity and guessing. Besides, if she is honest, she never has to worry about what she said.
- Date one guy at a time. Yes, all that attention can be flattering. But dating more than one guy at a time causes trouble and even fights. And remember this old saying, "Always leave the dance with the guy who brought you."
- Get advice from reliable sources about a guy you are interested in. Sometimes girlfriends are good, but males you trust are even better—they know things about other males that girls can't see.
- Dress appropriately. Males think differently than females do. Guys often judge the character of a girl by the clothes she wears (or doesn't wear).
- Don't become infatuated too quickly. Be patient. There are many good guys out there. Be choosy. Do not settle for second-best (or worse).
- Be yourself—males like authenticity.
- Guys don't like to talk about their feelings.

Females are wired to respond sexually when they receive non-sexual affection. Ideally, they receive this nonsexual affection from their fathers and develop a healthy self-image and self-esteem. But when fathers do not provide that healthy nonsexual affection that all girls crave, they tend to find it elsewhere. If you are overly critical of your daughter and never compliment her, what will happen the first time a boy compliments her? If you never tell her you love her, what will happen the first time a young man (especially if he is older) tells her he loves her? She needs to be aware of this proclivity and how her needs affect her judgment and the choices she makes.

Girls who do not get the healthy masculine affection they crave from their fathers go to great lengths and often make very poor choices in life to get it. They also tend to be very bitter toward men in general. Here is how one woman described her journey for the love she didn't get from her daddy:

> By this time I was a self-described, certifiable "Man Hater." I was so angry, bitter, and resentful. Every man I ever cared about cared more about alcohol than me. I decided "if you can't beat them, join them." I wanted to see what alcohol really had that was better than me. So I started drinking and I started drinking a lot! I started drinking every day after work and binge drinking on the weekends (when I didn't have my son). I drank beer, wine, shots, mixed drinks—whatever I could get. I was trying to become an alcoholic! How crazy is that? I was driving drunk, puking in bars, waking up in strange places. And I never quite felt *accomplished* unless I had "hooked up" in the process. I always felt I had it together enough to attract a man if I had hooked up the night before—even if I didn't remember it. I felt like I was always in control of everything and that felt good. For every man that I left the next day, I scored one for the girls' team. I wanted them to be the ones that felt used. I knew what I was doing was wrong, but I didn't care. The need and desire for a man's attention won every time.

Despite what they believe, girls and young women are vulnerable to the machinations and manipulations of boys and young men.

Because we were young men once, we understand how males think and act, and what their motives and modus operandi are. Fathers therefore are uniquely qualified to act as guardians of their daughters in this area. While moms might know more about what is going on inside a girl's head and what kind of tricks she might use to get her own way, dads know what is going on inside the young man waiting outside for her to sneak out her bedroom window at night.

Dating

The summer before she entered high school, Kelsey and I went on a weeklong road trip by ourselves. The trip was ostensibly to talk about high school, but I used it to talk about all the things she didn't want to know. Things like what teenage boys really want and how they think. Having her trapped in a car with Dad while crossing remote areas of eastern Washington allowed me to ramble on at will. The trip also allowed us to agree on some ground rules for the coming school year.

One of the things we settled on was that Kelsey would not date during her freshman year. Coming from a small private Christian school, this would allow her to get her feet on the ground and settle into public high school life. Kelsey honored our agreement with remarkably little resistance or complaining. I think she found it useful to be able to use Dad as an excuse to turn down the myriad of boys who descended upon her. It also allowed her to observe how boys react and how they think without the pressure of a relationship.

The next year she was able to slowly begin dating (if she wanted), starting out with group dates and then double dates. This again allowed her to gain experience without finding herself in an awkward position in which she would need to make a tough decision without the benefit of having been there before. Interestingly, she chose to not date until her junior year. Not because of lack of opportunities, but because she did not feel the overwhelming need to define her self-image by having a boy hold her hand in the hallways.

133

Other areas we agreed upon were that Kelsey would not call boys on the telephone, but she could receive calls from them. Boys need to learn to take the initiative in relationships and not be passive. Also, she could not date seniors until she was at least a junior. It is my opinion that boys at that age level are much too sophisticated in their manipulative abilities for young, inexperienced girls to deal with.

I also spent a good amount of time monitoring what my daughter wore in public. We all understand how visual males are. Have you noticed how some high school girls dress these days? Frankly, some of them look like hookers or strippers. What kind of message are these girls sending to males when they flaunt their bodies in that manner? I know the thoughts they evoke in me; I can only imagine what thoughts they produce in the mind of an eighteen-year-old male at the height of his sexual appetite. It's a miracle they get any schoolwork done. Whenever I see girls dressed like that, I always say to myself, "I wonder if her father knows she left the house dressed like that." I know many girls do change their clothes before getting to school. Maybe that's why dad should make an unscheduled visit to the school occasionally?

What to Bring on a Date

- Always have your own money in case you need to take a taxi or a bus home—that way you are not dependent upon your date.
- Have a fully charged cell phone in case you need to call your parents or a friend.
- Wear appropriate clothing.
- Carry a small canister of pepper spray and a light on your key chain.
- Always carry your ID with you.
- A small pocketknife is handy for many situations—you never need it until you need it.

Your daughter needs to be aware of the signals she sends out by the way she dresses. She might think that tight skimpy outfit makes her look cute, but when a man sees her in that outfit, he's picturing her naked. I think it was a bit shocking for my daughter to realize that once she went through puberty, *men*, not just boys, were attracted to her now. It lifted the bar on the playing field up to a whole new level. She was in the big leagues now, not just the minors anymore. Girls need to understand that their sexuality is not a toy; it is actually a powerful force that they need to treat with respect and responsibility. With great power comes the ability to cause great damage—to others and ourselves.

Dating Your Daughter

I always felt it was important to "date" my daughter to show her how she should be treated by another man. One of the first formal dates I took her on was when she turned twelve years old. I wanted it to be special, so we dressed up and I took her to an expensive steak house. During dinner I gave her a purity ring and talked about guys and the importance of keeping herself pure. Here was her recollection of that evening:

> Then, there was the time we went on that date to the fancy restaurant and had dinner. You were trying to teach me how to act on a date, napkin on the lap, all that stuff. And I personally had picked out what I thought was a gorgeous dark purple nail polish called something like Midnight Purple. Mom didn't like it and said it was way too dark (which it probably was) but you still said I looked very pretty. I remember sitting at the table and looking at my nails, thinking I agreed with mom and I probably shouldn't have worn that color, but again you still said I looked pretty. Taking me on dates like that to "learn" how to act was fun and helpful, but it was spending time with you that I liked the most. I know that's typical to say, but it meant more for me because even though mom didn't like my polish, you did.

Many women I've talked to either remembered warmly that their dads had dated them, or wished that they would have. One woman fondly described her experience like this:

When I was about twelve years old, Dad took me on my first date. He and Mom explained to me that this date was to teach me what a date *should* be like—how a young gentleman should behave, what a lady should expect, and what to do when those things didn't come about. I can't tell you that I had a problem-free dating situation; but while I was under my father's roof, he knew and had talked with every young man I went out with.

For that first date, Mom got me dressed up in a pretty party dress with my hair nicely brushed. Dad took me to a Chinese restaurant downtown. As a policeman, he'd walked a beat in that neighborhood. He'd saved the owners some money by preventing robberies, so they treated him like a king when we arrived. He taught me how to eat with chopsticks that night. It was magic!

Another woman had a very unique take on why a father should date his daughter:

Thinking through this made me wonder how many dads also "date" their daughters the way they dated their wives. Might sound weird, but think about it: you tried extra hard to understand her—you were taken with her and at some point knew she was the one for the rest of your life. A daughter is a "for the rest of your life" relationship. Do you work at getting to know your daughter and understand her the way you tried to get to know her mother when you were dating?

Wolves in Sheep's Clothing

The Bible likens families to flocks of sheep. Children, like lambs, are naive and simple in their understanding of the world. Fathers are like sheepdogs guarding the flock from marauding wolves. We protect our families from human predators, television programs, movies, music, books, corrupt friends, or any number of harmful people or influences that enter into a child's life.

By the way, it's fitting that sheepdogs come from the wolf genus, so they are no stranger to the wolves' traits and habits. Dads often find the hackles rising on our necks when we sense a wolf parading in sheep's clothing around our kids. I once told my teenage daughter, "I might not always know why, but I know a wolf when I see one; I can sense him." Of course, my daughter says that I think *all* boys are wolves, but I just tell her that's because I used to be one. It takes one to know one.

When I was dating, I was, like all young guys, deathly afraid of the fathers of the girls I went out with. If the majority of fathers showed any interest in meeting the boys their daughters were dating, I suspect that nearly all young men would be forced to remain celibate until marriage. Young men can show a lot of ingenuity when it comes to trying to bed a young woman. But since we've all been there before, we dads are uniquely suited to be the guard at the "palace gates," so to speak.

My friend Steve has two beautiful teenage daughters. Steve lives out in the country and is quite protective of his daughters. Late one night he heard a noise on his property and spotted in the distance what appeared to be a young man stumbling through the woods and working his way in the dark toward his daughters' bedroom window. Like any father with daughters, Steve promptly donned his night vision goggles, picked up his Winchester Model 870 12-gauge shotgun, and went to investigate. About fifty yards from the house, in complete darkness, Steve popped up out of the bushes, surprising the young man bent on having a moonlight rendezvous. As you can imagine, the young man nearly soiled himself while frantically trying to explain why he was trespassing on private property, all the while staring down the barrel of a shotgun wielded by a slightly crazed person who resembled a frogman. Needless to say, Steve never had any midnight visits again after word spread of this encounter.

As men we have the ability to detect things about other men. Because of our instincts we can detect things about males that women can't. Recently my wife and I were attending a peaceful

Tea Party rally to protest government overspending. (No, despite what the mainstream media promotes about Tea Party members, I am not a racist.) A young man approached us with a little girl on his shoulders and proceeded to ask my wife questions about what she believed and what her concerns were. It quickly became apparent to me that his actual intent was to very subtly make her look stupid and incompetent. He was using the little girl not only as protection against another man punching him in the nose, but also to trick women into lowering their defenses by subconsciously appealing to their mothering instincts. He was actually an infiltrator with a hidden camera who was determined to make the protesters look bad.

Even as I stepped in and told him to take a hike, my wife thought I was being rude and did not glean his actual intent. It was only after she watched him interact with other women in the crowd (whose menfolk also ran him off) that she recognized how he had pulled the wool over her eyes. Once he was "found out," the man proceeded to be adversarial and aggressive. It was a cowardly display on his part, but it illustrates how trusting women can be.

Guard Dog or Shepherd?

I wanted the boys hanging around my daughter to think of me as a leathery old Marine master sergeant (picture Clint Eastwood in *Heartbreak Ridge*). They should think of me as tough, slightly crazy (or at least unpredictable), and demanding. The likely candidates would have to get through me first in order to have a chance at the prize, with only the most worthy passing muster.

If you are a hunter, let your daughter's dates know that. They need to know you have guns and are not afraid to use them. I kept a mounted rack of mule deer antlers on the wall. A visual aid like that might be just the thing a young man needs to cool his ardor during the heat of passion. Author Meg Meeker shares this about her dad:

He was a hunter and he let my boyfriends know that. They saw the moose head on the wall as they entered our house and my dad made sure they knew who put the head up there. He thought he was being funny; I thought he was embarrassing me. But he protected me, not from predatory boys or monsters, but from myself. I was young and too trusting of people and he knew that long before I did.[2]

My daughter dated a variety of knuckleheads during her teenage years. Despite my active presence and involvement, she still managed to sneak a few "slick Willies" past me. Most of them didn't last long, but like a lot of girls, she was attracted to certain types of "bad boys." Many of you guys out there who think your daughters would never do anything so foolish are either fooling yourselves or are in for a big surprise. It's amazing how resourceful young women can be at hiding this kind of thing from their fathers.

One night Kelsey did not come home by her curfew. Since I always waited up for her when she was out, I found myself pacing the floor as the hours went by. Numerous calls to her cell phone went directly to voice mail. Finally, at four o'clock in the morning, I got a call from a scared little girl saying, "Daddy, we got stuck on top of Larch Mountain in the snow. Can you come and get me please?" Stuffing my anger beneath my concern for her safety, I quickly drove the twenty-some miles into the forest until I finally found them alongside the snow-covered winding road leading up the mountainside.

Apparently they had slipped the chain closing the road and decided it would be fun to drive up to the lookout. After getting up there, the young man thought he would impress her by spinning "cookies" in the parking area. Unfortunately, he failed to consider that his two-wheel-drive compact would not have any traction in the snow. His car ended up precariously perched halfway over a cliff with a two-hundred-foot drop below. Luckily a tree had stopped their downward descent. My daughter had been forced to walk several miles down the access road in order to get cell phone service.

Needless to say, I had a few things to say on the ride home. I don't think we ever saw that young man again. As an aside, here's how sharp this young guy was: he carried around the title to his car in the car's glove compartment. When I asked him why, he said, "So I can find it."

My role as Kelsey's guard dog required me to run off many wolves who were circling her. That required a lot of work and diligence on my part. I wasn't always perfect, but I did persevere even when I failed.

As a side note here, let me say that I think it is important that you have an established curfew for your daughter. That curfew time changed in our home depending upon whether it was a school night or the weekend. It also changed as Kelsey got older and showed more responsibility. Even after she graduated from high school and lived at home as a young adult, she was still subject to a curfew. She didn't always like it, but as long as she was in my home, she was subject to my rules. Like all kids, she tried protesting her curfew with the old "Anything you can do at 2:00 a.m. you can do at 10:00 p.m." line. However, it's been my experience that nothing good ever happens out there after midnight. That is when the "night people" take over and the world changes.

One area we as fathers should be aware of is the influences in the lives of the young men who hang around our daughters. I always wanted to meet their fathers and mothers. I also wanted to see what their friends were like. This was part of my role as shepherd. The truth is, a young man is almost always influenced by the mentors in his life. Not that a boy's past is his future; it's just that the influence of masculine role models plays a big part in the type of man he becomes and the behaviors he emulates.

I served in the US Navy as a boiler technician aboard a ship in the mid to late 1970s. Shortly before I came on board the ship, another man was assigned to the fire room as well. He was slightly older than the other young men and obviously more worldly than most.

A rather handsome man and the sort that a certain kind of woman is attracted to, he considered himself a ladies man. His "Don Juan" attitude became a bit of a joke among the sailors, who did not take him as seriously as he took himself. But I watched over the years as several young men came on board, fresh-faced and naive, and fell under his influence. These young men, most of them eager and somewhat innocent, were impressed with his panache and joie de vivre. He made it his mission to "mentor" these young men into learning how to dress, act, and speak in a way appealing to women, with the goal of bedding them. Interestingly enough, his methods were quite effective, and after a relatively short period of time, we had three or four little Romeos swaggering about the ship.

I found myself wondering recently (thirty years later—you don't need to hit me in the head with a two-by-four) whether these young men were permanently changed by this experience. Were these innocent young men tainted so that they spent the rest of their lives as womanizers? They seemed so fresh and innocent with great potential prior to this man's mentoring. As the father of a young adult son who is still a bit naive of the ways of the world, I would be devastated if another man came along and used his influence to ruin my son's character to such a degree. And what about all this from my daughter's perspective? How many men like this are produced worldwide by those who pass along the worst masculine traits from mentor to mentee, from father to son? What type of men is she exposed to if enough males are formed in this way?

Respect

I recently rewatched (for about the tenth time) the classic movie *The Godfather* (even as I write this the theme music is playing in my head). I was struck in this particular viewing by the level of respect a young man is required to demonstrate to a girl's father if he wants to court her. In one scene when Michael Corleone is hiding in Sicily, he is thunderstruck by a young beauty (Apollonia) he sees in the countryside. After inadvertently offending her café-owning father by inquiring about her availability, Corleone goes to great lengths to apologize, and he asks very respectfully if he may court his daughter: "I apologize if I offended you. I am a stranger in this country. And I meant no disrespect to you, or your daughter. I am an American, hiding in Sicily. My name is Michael Corleone. There are people who'd pay a lot of money for that information. But then your daughter would lose a father instead of gaining a husband. I wanna meet your daughter with your permission and under the supervision of your family with all respect."

Surely if a high-ranking mafioso can be that respectful, the young punks circling my daughter can show some respect. Today, it seems like being disrespectful is a requirement for young men. It irritates me to have the geeky young clerks at Best Buy come up and address me as "bud" or "dude" or even "boss." I'm a military veteran, I'm a published author, I have owned a successful business for over twenty years, I've been married for twenty-nine years and raised two children to healthy adulthood. I think I've earned the right to be called "sir," not "chief." Well, now I just *sound* like some old curmudgeon, but I think you get my point. I understand now what all those old guys were mad about when I was a young punk.

Recently, Lt. Colonel (Ret.) Oliver North spoke at our church. Everyone laughed when he said that he still makes all of his sons-in-law call him "Colonel." But he said it establishes respect, authority, and the proper chain of command. When boyfriends (and even husbands) respect a woman's father, it garners respect for the woman as well. It also provides authority and accountability in those younger men's lives. Young men who respect a girl's father are more likely to respect her as well.

At this point in time, my daughter has been dating a young man for about a year. He still calls me Mr. Johnson. I have not yet dissuaded him of that notion. Am I being a bit of a jerk about it?

Probably—but it is important to me that he show me respect as a precursor to loving my daughter. She means too much to me to give her away to someone who cannot or will not appreciate and cherish her. Since men seldom appreciate anything that comes cheap, if nothing else, this is a way of making him feel like he is working hard to earn a prize.

FOR DISCUSSION AND REFLECTION

- Dads have a great deal of wisdom about boys that can be beneficial to their daughters. But not if he doesn't share it! What is a good age to start talking to your daughter about boys? (Hint: When she enters puberty is probably long past the time.)

- Why do girls need to understand what drives males and some of the differences between males and females, especially as boys enter puberty?

- How can we best teach our daughters how a male should treat her?

- What are some ways to model that lesson for her?

- Have you prepared your daughter for dating?

- What rules and guidelines will you set in place?

9

Uh-Oh! She's Becoming a Woman!

My eleven-year-old daughter mopes around the house all day waiting for her breasts to grow.

Bill Cosby

I remember the first time I saw my "little princess" walk down the stairs in a prom dress with heels, her hair in an updo and makeup on her face. The first time that happens, it's like time suddenly stands still and the realization punches you in the gut that your precious little baby girl has somehow stepped through the looking glass and come out the other side as a young woman. In the blink of an eye my little baby girl had become a woman.

Seemingly overnight your daughter changes from your sweet little princess into an awkward, knobby-kneed tween before finally morphing into a fully-developed young woman—all in a few short years. But don't be fooled. She may look like a twenty-five-year-old on the outside, but inside she is really still a little girl. Psychologically, emotionally, and intellectually, she is a girl trapped in a woman's body. The physical changes she undergoes often fool her and the world into thinking she is more mature than she really is.

The following are some areas that your daughter needs to be prepared for and in which a loving father can best supply information.

Sexuality

Teenage girls of a certain age are heartbreakers for their fathers. Here is this sweet little baby girl whom you love with all your heart. All you really care about is her safety. You would gladly die for her. But in her headlong rush to jump into life, she could care less about your heart. You are perceived by your daughter as the authority in the home whether you want that role or not. Even good girls feel compelled to rebel at some point in their teen years. Here's how one young woman explained it:

> First off my dad was a pastor, so that kind of put a spin on everything. I felt such a huge need to rebel and prove to everyone that we weren't perfect that it affected my teen years so deeply. My poor dad even had to go before the board and ask if he should resign because of all my trouble. He was my world though. And when I got caught I would cry not because I was afraid of his punishments but because I was so sad that I would break his heart again.

Girls and young women have so much garbage shoved at them every minute of every day. Our kids are being sexualized at ever younger ages. Girls are encouraged at younger and younger ages to have breast implants, Botox injections in their lips, and plastic surgery to correct any minor physical imperfections. Their role models are young female singers who parade around nearly naked on videos simulating eroticism, group sex, homosexuality, bondage, and sadomasochism. Images of female models on TV and in magazines are Photoshopped to look more voluptuous and desirable than is humanly possible. These images create impossible standards for girls and take a toll on our young women. Many girls resort to eating disorders, cutting themselves, and therapy to cope with the psychological pressures of wanting to have a physical appearance that is literally unattainable.

The sexualization of our children permeates every media outlet of our culture, from department store ads in the newspaper to music videos to movies and television. Our culture pressures girls to have sex at younger ages. If a girl is not sexually active, she will often be teased as a social outcast by her peers. But this early indoctrination into the world of sex can have devastating consequences on her psyche. Meg Meeker explains,

> I see this all the time in young girls. When they first try sex—not necessarily intercourse—they are curious and usually very disappointed. The disappointment makes them feel that something is wrong with them, because everyone else says it's great. So they try again and again. In very short order they become emotionally dulled. Their instincts tell them that intimacy with another person has occurred, but their mind senses that no love was exchanged, no commitment was made, no emotional depth was involved. They become confused about love because sex came before love.[1]

Michael Gurian says, "To put this more plainly, adolescent girls often feel driven to do whatever it takes to get the affection of someone who is attaching to them."[2]

A father plays a big role in determining a girl's sexuality and the sexual decisions she makes. Talk with your daughter about girls you knew growing up who were considered malleable or easily manipulated into compromising their virtue for the affection and attention of boys. Discuss whether your daughter thinks those girls were happy and what challenges they faced. One of the topics we discussed often with our daughter in high school was the statistical outcomes of girls from fatherless homes (many of my daughter's friends came from that situation). While we confirmed that a person's past is certainly not their future, girls from fatherless homes are statistically more likely to be promiscuous, have more sexual partners, and have a higher rate of unwed teen pregnancies.

Her Virtue

There's an old saying that goes, "A father is more effective than any condom at preventing pregnancy." The father with a shotgun standing in front of his virginal daughter to protect her virtue from the traveling salesman is a long-standing stereotype. But like many stereotypes, the reason so many people can relate to it is because there is some kernel of truth to it. As fathers we are programmed in our DNA to know that part of our role is to protect our daughters' virtue. That directive is what helped civilization grow—it kept girls from being abused incestuously or from being physically damaged. It also ensured that decent men carried forward the seeds of procreation and not men who would abandon, abuse, or even kill their offspring. Today some men may disregard that impulse or be intimidated into stifling it, but we all feel the compulsion to protect our daughters. And in fact because so many men are shying away from that directive, we are seeing the consequences in our culture of women bearing children by men who do not stay and nurture them physically, emotionally, and financially.

Give your daughter *permission* to wait to have sex. Much of the world is pushing her to become sexually active. Her father's voice has great power in this arena. Tell her that it is okay to wait, and that in fact it is best to wait until she is married. She needs her father's perspective, encouragement, and even permission in order to be able to resist the many temptations she will be faced with while growing up.

Even though our culture ridicules it, there are many benefits to a girl's guarding her virtue. The benefits of a good reputation are multifold. Proverbs 22:1 says, "A good name is more desirable than great riches; to be esteemed is better than silver or gold." Besides, studies show that girls who wait to have sex tend to enjoy sex more and have a more fulfilling marriage.

Early Development

Girls mature mentally, emotionally, and physically more quickly than boys. That means a young woman in puberty is often attracted to young men two or more years older than she is. Yikes! That sends shivers down my spine just thinking about how naive and vulnerable young girls are at that age. But girls who develop physically early in life face even more challenges. They are generally less happy with their bodies when they get older than girls who develop later in adolescence. Girls who develop later than their peers also face some challenges but are generally better off emotionally and psychologically.

The most recent in a flood of studies over the past decade confirms that girls are entering puberty at younger ages than in the past. The study confirmed that girls are more likely today than in the past to start developing breasts by age seven or eight. The study, conducted within the Breast Cancer and the Environment Research Centers (BCERC), in partnership with the National Institute of Environmental Health Science and the National Cancer Institute, found that at age eight, 18 percent of Caucasian, 43 percent of African American, and 31 percent of Latino girls had enough breast development to be considered at the onset of puberty.[3]

However, it appears that girls who have healthy relationships with their fathers actually enter puberty later than girls who are fatherless.[4] When girls are raised in homes where men who are biologically unrelated to them are frequent occupants, it appears to induce them to enter puberty at an earlier age. One in six girls in Britain now enters puberty by eight years of age, according to recent research. This compares with one in one hundred a generation ago. "Girls are now having sex before their great-great-grandmothers had their first period. Half of all girls in Britain will have entered puberty by the age of ten," announced Professor Jane Golding, director of the study at Bristol University's Institute of Child Health last June after tracking the development of 14,000 children from birth. In North America, one in seven Caucasian girls and almost half of African American girls enter puberty (develop breasts or pubic hair) by the age of eight.[5]

There are a variety of causes for this, including heavier prepubescent weight, hormones used in pesticides on fruits and vegetables, and growth hormones used in meat and poultry. But another significant contributing factor may be because girls who are around unrelated men (such as boyfriends and live-in lovers) produce more pheromones, which in turn launch them into puberty, possibly as a natural defense mechanism in case of sexual activity or molestation.

If your daughter does develop early, do what you can to help her discourage the attention of older boys and men. While she might be flattered by their attention, she is not equipped emotionally or psychologically to deal with older males who often view her as a woman and not a little girl. Start by teaching her to dress modestly. Next talk to her openly and honestly about the biological drive that young males have to engage in sex. Teach her that many males will say or do anything in order to fulfill that drive. While it might be a tad uncomfortable to talk about it, she needs to understand how males think and why. What better source to get accurate information from than her father?

A Father's Influence in Sexual Decision Making

Sex is a taboo subject in much of the Christian world, especially as far as our young single women are concerned. Probably all parents, Christian or not, desire for their children to remain sexually pure until marriage. However, the reality is that young people today face sexual temptations most of their parents never encountered and probably cannot fathom. In addition, most of our young people will fail to remain celibate until marriage.

By the twelfth grade, 62 percent of teenagers have had sexual intercourse.[6] The average age of first sexual intercourse is now seventeen.[7] By extrapolation we can conclude that a significant number of teenagers in the church also will have engaged in this behavior long before they are married. Interestingly, a study showed that 76 percent of teen girls said their fathers influenced their decisions on whether or not they should become sexually active.[8] And 97 percent of girls who said they could talk to their parents had lower teen pregnancy rates.[9]

Casual sex and promiscuity often have devastating effects on a woman's psyche. The consequences to her body and emotional health aren't always apparent until years later. The physical health risks alone are enough to warrant caution. The wide variety of sexually transmitted diseases (STDs) and other potential health risks from birth control and abortion have been documented in numerous studies. Legalized abortions upon demand, a by-product of the sexual revolution, have been proven to be physically, psychologically, emotionally, and spiritually damaging to women (not to mention the unborn child).

Currently 34 percent of all young women in this country will get pregnant at least once before the age of twenty. Of these pregnancies, eight out of ten are unintended and 81 percent of them involve unmarried teens.[10] Only one-third of teen mothers will obtain a high school diploma, and only 1.5 percent will get a college degree by the time they are thirty years old.[11] Those numbers do not bode well as a predictor for a successful life for a woman or her children.

Other more lethal consequences to promiscuous sexual behavior loom as an even larger threat to women. The statistics regarding STDs are staggering. It is estimated that 25 percent of sexually active teens currently have an STD or a sexually transmitted infection (STI). Many are not aware of it. Basically, if you sleep with someone, you are sleeping with every person they slept with and every person each of those people slept with. You see how STDs can spread exponentially among the population. The only way to ensure that you do not acquire an STD is to practice abstinence. Condoms do not prevent many of the sexual diseases that are rampaging through the community.

About four million teens contract an STD each year.[12] The often fatal AIDS and HIV epidemic in this country and around the world speaks to the dangers of irresponsible sexual activity. But there are a host of other STDs, several of which are incurable and do great damage to a woman's body. The possible consequences from STDs include infertility, a greater risk for certain types of cancer, brain damage, heart disease, birth defects, and even death.

Women who enter into sexual relations too early in a relationship also tend to place more significance on the relationship than it deserves. This leads to trouble in that they continue in unhealthy relationships because they have already sacrificed or invested a valuable portion of themselves.

I'm convinced that when we remain sexually pure until marriage, God blesses our sexual union. We appreciate more what we have been given. And like everything in life, humans appreciate and value things that they've worked hard and struggled for more than what they are given easily.

Because of the way I was raised, I did not understand the value of remaining sexually pure until marriage. I now recognize the wisdom (on so many levels) of delayed gratification in this area; however, because of our cultural bent, I can imagine it must be very difficult for young people today to grasp the significance of this principle. As a father you can help your daughter immeasurably by helping her understand why this is important and the value that God places on this act of dedication. I truly believe God blesses those who wait in many ways, not the least of which is giving a couple a greater degree of intimacy, a more enjoyable love life, and a stronger bond of marriage.

Having sex with another person gives a part of you to that person. When we give pieces of ourselves to others before marriage, we create a legacy that drains some of our "sexual essence." We leave residual intimacy with all of our former partners and keep some of their residue in us. Women, with their natural desire for intimacy, are hurt most by intimate relations in situations that don't last, especially when they have given away precious pieces of their souls. Why do you think prostitutes look so hard and used up at such a young age? Believe me, they don't look (or act) like Julia Roberts in the movie *Pretty Woman*. Certainly their lifestyle is partly to blame, but I think the fracturing and loss of so many pieces of their soul to so many men plays a significant role as well.

One woman described the painful effect of her father's absence on her sexuality this way:

> I lost my virginity at the age of fourteen. By the time I graduated from high school, I had slept with ten boys. I was smoking pot, drinking, and doing other drugs. At nineteen, I met a guy at a party, had sex with him, and ended up pregnant. I was still living at home. Since my mom worked so much, I had little to no supervision. Half the boys I slept with were in my bedroom, just down the hall from mom. I snuck them in at night and out before dawn. Somewhere around my very early twenties, I just woke up and realized what a piece of crap my dad really was. I realized that my mom made the right choice by leaving him all those years ago, and I felt silly for crying myself to sleep all those nights because I wanted my parents back together. By now I learned very quickly that I could get boys' attention by sleeping with them. During the "chase" I remember always feeling needed, beautiful, attractive, desired. Even if it was a one-night stand, it felt good to know that this "man" desired me enough to give me his time.

Imagine how it would feel if it was your daughter who had written that statement. As fathers we must recognize the pain and destruction we cause through our remoteness and uninvolvement in our daughters' lives.

Even though as a father you do not have the ultimate control over your daughter's body, it is important for her to understand your feelings about how she uses it. This woman's story touches every father's heart:

> On one of these dates, when I was sixteen, he told me he wanted us to be closer and really talk. See, one of my biggest regrets with my parents was that I never felt like I could truly be me. Be the *real* me. They were so good, and so pure. Met as young teens, they were each other's first and only loves, waited to have sex till marriage, and never watched R-rated movies. Never did drugs or drank and so on, and so they would never understand me. So, our relationship was built on a lot of lies. I so wanted to talk about real life issues with them, but knew they wouldn't be able to take it. So on this particular date, my dad is saying, "Let's talk" so I do. I tell him that I lost my virginity at fifteen, and there in the middle of the restaurant he begins to sob. Deep, sad tears. I broke his heart once again. He wasn't mad, he didn't yell, he just cried. He was so sad for me. I had a whole list of things I was going to tell him, but seeing how deeply I had hurt him, I changed my mind and when he asked if there was more, I told him no. It killed me to hurt him.

Talk to your daughter often about this issue. I'm not sure that young women in our culture are taught to truly understand the value of their virtue and the harm that comes from disregarding it so freely. Even if it hurts, it is vitally important that a girl has a father who loves, supports, and especially forgives her.

Dating and the Vetting Process

As a man, and a dad of a daughter, I am familiar with all the male codes of conduct and unwritten rules regarding women. Hence it is my duty to protect my daughter as best as I can. I did this in several ways when Kelsey was in high school. Since first impressions are important, I always wanted to leave a lasting memory during the first meeting with one of her suitors. Besides cleaning my handgun, scowling at him, and crushing his hand during the greeting, I also instituted the infamous "have lunch with dad" policy. I believe this policy became well-known around the high school during the years my daughter attended. If a boy looked like he was going to be sniffing around, my daughter would casually tell him that one of the requirements to date her was that he had to call me and schedule a lunch date. That in and of itself ran off many weak-willed young men or ne'er-do-wells. This luncheon gave me the opportunity to assess the young man's character, to find out facts about his background (so I could track him down if I had to), and also to instill some rules regarding dating my daughter. My reputation soon preceded me. One young man who had a longtime crush on Kelsey finally asked her to dinner. She replied, "You mean like a date?"

After a brief pause he responded, "No, I don't think I'm quite ready yet to have lunch with your dad."

When Kelsey was nineteen years old, she was living in her own apartment. She was home visiting one day and was telling me about all the young men who were enamored with her and wanted to date her. I somewhat jokingly suggested she have the young men call me to schedule a lunch. But after thinking about it a moment, I told her, "Kelsey, you are nineteen years old now, an adult living on your own. I guess you don't need me to interview your dates any longer."

She thought about it for a minute and said, "That's okay—you can still do it!" As I mentally pumped my fist in the air, *my* heart swelled to realize that I had gotten it right. She saw the value of having a father who loved her and was willing to protect her. I can only imagine the feelings of safety and security that produces in a young woman.

Dating Tips for You

Dating for a young woman, especially one still under the gentle protection of a loving mother and father, provides a training ground for her to learn about relationships, the opposite sex, and her own feelings and decision-making processes. If done properly and with restraint, it allows her to stretch her boundaries and mature at an acceptable, safe pace. Unfortunately, many young women, in their hurry to grow up, rush through this natural process. Some disregard their parents' wishes, or worse, lack the protection and guidance of an involved father.

One of the first steps your daughter should make a priority before dating is to pray for God to direct her into the right relationships. Then have her set physical and emotional boundaries *before* they are put to the test. Have her talk about those boundaries to friends or parents so she establishes some accountability for herself. Being in the throes of passion is not a good time to try and decide how far you want to go or where to draw the line on a physical level. That's how unwanted pregnancies occur. "I didn't mean to get pregnant—it just happened! It was an accident!"

If your daughter still lives at home, make sure you meet all of her dates right from the very beginning. She probably already knows she is making a poor and potentially dangerous choice if she is ashamed to bring a young man around because she knows you wouldn't approve of him.

In the not-so-distant "old days," young men were required to ask a girl's father for permission to date her. This served the purpose of establishing the father's authority and it set the tone for the relationship. Young men who have met a girl's father and spent some time alone with him tend to be more cautious and respectful of her. Either that or they disappear in short order, searching for easier prey without that layer of protection.

Dating Tips for Your Daughter

Have your daughter consider keeping her first few dates with a young man limited to daytime events. I would also encourage her, at least for a while, to only go out with him in places where there are crowds of people. This gives her a chance to get to know him a little before trusting him with her safety. If your daughter still lives at home, make sure he understands the importance of getting her home on time after each date. This shows respect for her and her parents. I was a stickler on making sure my daughter got home on time. I would usually tell the young man something like this before they left the house: "You know Kelsey's curfew is midnight, right? And I consider you personally responsible to make sure she gets home safely by that time."

Make your daughter have boys telephone her—she shouldn't call them. That serves the purpose of keeping a male from being passive. He needs to work and be the aggressor in the relationship. If a male knows a girl is sitting around pining away for him, he will start taking her for granted. Also, make sure he comes to the door to pick her up and that he always opens the car door for her.

If your daughter is even slightly serious about a young man, she should get to know his family and family background. (In fact, you should get to know his family as well.) How is love and affection shown in his family? How is anger expressed? What role does the young man play in his family? What type of generational sin runs through his family (favoritism, alcoholism, fatherlessness, abandonment, abuse, and so forth)? Again, men can change—no one's past is his destiny. However, change takes desire, knowledge, hard work, and awareness. But it has been my experience that people generally do not change without God's intervention. A young woman and her prospective mate need to understand what challenges they face and will need to help each other overcome. It also helps her be aware of what she might be up against should she decide to enter into a deeper relationship with this person.

Lastly, teach your daughter to insist that a date treat her with respect from the beginning. If she respects herself, he will too. He needs to work for her favor in order to truly appreciate how wonderful she is. When she establishes this level of respect in a relationship from the beginning, it sets the tone for the future. Obviously she won't know at the beginning if this is the man she wants to spend her life with or not, but if he is, it's best to have that standard set in place for the rest of their lives together.

Sex Education—Talk to Her

Being a father never seems to be easy. In fact as your kids get older, it gets even harder in certain areas. One of those difficult areas involves sex.

Our culture is such now that junior high students routinely engage in oral sex (the sixth-grade daughter of my friend recently told him she had been approached by three boys at school to have oral sex, including one from her church youth group), trade nude photos of each other in cyberspace, and engage in lewd "grinding" dancing resembling dry sex. High school and college students have a hookup culture called "friends with benefits." This means there is no intimate relationship (or any relationship at all) beyond occasionally indulging in sexual intercourse with each other. One young woman was hurt deeply when during a time of loneliness she contacted her "friend" for support and companionship and was told, "Sorry, ours is just a sexual relationship—there're no strings attached." She finally realized that in this kind of arrangement he was the only friend receiving all the benefits. This kind of sexual indoctrination has some pretty significant consequences for young people and for our culture as well.

With all the negative outcomes regarding promiscuous sexuality, it is especially important that our teenagers be properly educated about the dangers involved. But it's difficult talking to your kids about sex. Especially for dads, talking with teenage girls about their sexuality can be a pretty intimidating task. That's why many parents today leave sexual education to the schools. But because it's tough is precisely why it's our duty as parents to teach our sons and daughters about sexual purity.

The problem with allowing others—like public schools—to educate our children is that their values may not correspond with ours. Abstinence training has fallen out of favor with a more liberal administration taking over federal funding, and groups like Planned Parenthood have eagerly stepped in to fill the gap. The problem with their philosophy is that even the way they teach abstinence is probably shocking to most parents. Comprehensive sex education, one of the more popular curriculums in public school districts across the country, teaches abstinence by having small coed groups of sixth to eighth graders get together and study a list of sexual behaviors such as anal intercourse, mutual masturbation, and oral sex to determine a consensus on what *they* consider to be abstinence. It seems very embarrassing and humiliating for a twelve- or thirteen-year-old girl to have to discuss these kinds of activities with a group of boys. Most dads I know wouldn't want their young daughters talking about that kind of stuff with young males.

Talking about sex can be daunting. As we men all know, the four words that strike fear into our hearts is to have our wives say "We need to talk." Even worse is to have your wife *and* your daughter approach you with that directive.

One day I was relaxing in my easy chair, minding my own business, enjoying the football game on TV. Suddenly, my wife and daughter bustled into the room on a mission and announced, "We need to talk." First of all, not being prepared to enter into a verbal conversation was daunting enough. But the intensity of their expressions put even more pressure on me to perform. I was smart enough to know that I needed (albeit reluctantly) to turn off the TV. At my wife's prompting, Kelsey proceeded to explain that she had been dating her boyfriend for two years. She felt she really loved him and thought perhaps for his nineteenth birthday she would like to give him a gift. You know—THE gift! Of course, a verbal barrage of exclamations and shouting started from both women. It was similar to being caught between a warship and a castle, both firing their cannons at each other at will.

Using that distraction as a time to think (and pray) allowed me to assess the situation. My first impulse was to say, "If you're asking for my permission, the answer is no." But after calming my wife down, I briefly reviewed with Kelsey the many discussions we'd had regarding our views on the emotional, psychological, and physical benefits of remaining sexually pure until marriage. Since she was a bit ambiguous about the church at that time, it didn't seem like a good time to bring up the moral aspects of the issue—not if I wanted her to keep an open mind.

I then conceded that she was of legal age to engage in that behavior if she wanted. But I also explained that while she was living under my roof, I was still responsible (and accountable to God) for her actions. We then at length logically discussed the positive and negative consequences of following through with that plan of action. As you might expect, the list was heavily weighted on the negative consequences side of the paper. I concluded by telling her that her boyfriend was welcome to call me, and if he could convince me it was a good idea, I would be happy to give it my blessing.

Frankly, I don't know for sure what Kelsey decided, but I did feel good that she was comfortable enough to come to me and her mother for advice. Had I exploded and forbidden her to even think about something like this, I expect it would have had the opposite effect that I wanted. She would have probably followed through if for no other reason than rebellion.

If you start early and can become comfortable discussing these issues before puberty sets in, you're the best person to introduce your daughter to a subject that she will deal with for her entire lifetime. She *will* go through puberty and *will* have many questions. Wouldn't you rather your daughter get the answers to those questions from you than from the guy down the street—or worse yet, from the secular entertainment industry? Talking about sex early and often while your children are growing up gets them comfortable talking with you about it when it really counts—as they get to be teenagers.

Talk to them beginning when they are young and talk to them often over the years about this subject. They will let you know what they are comfortable talking about. Speak as matter-of-factly as you can. Don't use pet names for body parts, even at an early age. The key is to get them comfortable talking with you about this subject *before* it becomes necessary.

It is also important to talk with them about the stages they will go through *before* they enter that stage. For instance, waiting to talk with your daughter about her period until *after* she starts is probably not a smart way to approach this subject. I know, if you're like me, that's the absolute last subject you want to talk about with your daughter. But if she does not have a mother, she needs someone who loves her to talk about one of the most important changes that a girl goes through.

As a parent, your wisdom and life experience are some of the most valuable contributions you can pass on to your children. The mistakes you've made in this area can help keep your daughter (or son) from making the same mistakes—but not if you don't share them.

FOR DISCUSSION AND REFLECTION

• Are you prepared for the physical and emotional changes your darling baby girl is going to go through in puberty? I know you *think* you are, but ask some fathers of older daughters what the most challenging aspects to that season of life were.

• Why are boundaries important in a girl's life, and why is it important that her father hold firm to those boundaries?

- How do you as a father influence your daughter's sexuality and her sexual decision-making process?

- Make a commitment with other men to all interview your daughters' dates before they go out with them—it's important! What do you think that encounter will be like? Probably a bit uncomfortable for you—but even more so for the young man.

10

Character Training

When our children were eight and ten years old, we took a vacation to Puerto Vallarta, Mexico. One day we decided to take a guided snorkeling cruise. As is the custom on these cruises, the crew of the boat was plying the male tourists with tequila shooters. Because I seldom drink alcohol anyway (especially at nine o'clock in the morning), I refused their offers even though most of the other men were steadily accepting the free refreshments. Perhaps the crew considered my refusals a challenge, because they stepped up their efforts to get me to take a drink. They became quite aggressive, even going so far as to jokingly question my manhood. Frankly, after so much steady pressure they started to wear me down, and I thought to myself, "What the heck, I'm on vacation. What's wrong with taking one drink?"

Fortunately, just as I was about to cave in, I looked around and saw two sets of little round, wide eyeballs watching me intently. Given that my wife and I had spent the better part of our kids' childhood telling them the merits of resisting peer pressure, it didn't seem like a good time to demonstrate just the opposite in front of them, and so I firmly refused any further attempts to solicit me with libations. I shiver to think that one moment of weakness on my part could have ruined all our hard efforts to teach them a valuable character trait. Had they witnessed my succumbing to peer pressure, nothing I said on the subject would have counted after that. Perhaps nothing I said on any subject would have carried much weight after that.

One thing we must remember is that our children will always imitate what we *do*, not what we *say* to do. Unfortunately, they always seem to imitate our worst traits instead of our best. Because of that tendency we need to constantly be aware of the example of character we set for them.

Additionally, character and morality are areas where your daughter needs healthy female mentors. This is especially true during adolescence. A girl often listens to a mentor with rapt attention, though the exact same teaching from her parents falls on deaf ears. In the past this mentoring role was fulfilled by grandmothers, aunts, godmothers, and family friends. Today, you need to be more intentional in finding good role models and mentors to speak into your daughter's life.

It's important for your daughter to know that a good reputation is difficult to get and easy to lose, but a bad reputation is easy to get and difficult to lose. Your daughter will face many different kinds of challenges throughout her life. Her success (and her reputation) will partly be determined by how she meets these challenges. The character that she has will be an important factor in meeting these challenges successfully. One of the biggest influences in how she develops that character will be what her father models for her.

Traits attributed to women of character—especially the biblical examples of femininity—include kindness, discretion, diligence, respectability, inner strength and beauty, grace, trustworthiness, wisdom, financial prudence, generosity, and compassion. Let's look at some character traits that fathers can intentionally instill in their daughters.

Character Traits All Girls Need

Life is hard. It is a series of struggles. That's just the way it is. I wonder if God didn't make life that way in order to develop our character. God seems to be more concerned with our character than he is with our comfort. Those who are best equipped to deal with the difficulties of life have a much better chance of living healthy, happy, satisfied lives. One of the major hurdles I remember facing from being raised in an alcoholic, dysfunctional home was learning how to solve life's challenges. The best system I found for healthy advice and wisdom came from the Bible.

The Judeo-Christian belief system has arguably done more to promote equality between the sexes than any other institution since the beginning of civilization. Prior to Christ's appearance and teachings, women were little more than chattel, virtually owned by their fathers and husbands. Even aristocratic Roman women, the most liberated women in the history of the world to that point, only had rights through their husbands. They could not own land, they were not allowed to drink wine, and they couldn't vote or participate in government. They couldn't even have a personal name but had to take a feminine form of their father's middle name.

The Bible was perhaps the first book that celebrated the character of women. Ruth was "a woman of noble character" (Ruth 3:11). Deborah was a wise judge with power over all the land. Her wisdom won a great victory in battle for her people. Esther saved thousands of her people's lives through her wisdom and courage. Lydia, a wealthy businesswoman, was one of the first converts to Christianity and a financial supporter and leader of the early church.

Biblical character training helps our daughters develop a moral-based or character-based self-esteem as opposed to a feeling-based self-esteem. With that in mind, let's discuss some character traits that I think all fathers would like their daughters to have in order to succeed in life.

Courage

My daughter is one of the bravest people I've ever met. Kelsey was born with a bilateral cleft lip. Her upper lip was open from the lip all the way up to her nose, having never formed together in two separate places. She has undergone six surgeries—the first at two months of age. If she was ever scared going into surgery, she never showed it. By the age of fifteen she had developed into a gorgeous young lady. (Funny how God works, isn't it?) However, even now she still has noticeable scars on her lip. Our family doesn't notice them, but rest assured Kelsey does—especially through all the angst and self-consciousness of her teenage years. Yet she's never let it keep her from doing whatever she wants. She continues to expose herself to vulnerable situations such as trying out for different sports, seeking out church activities, going to new schools, and attending summer camps—usually places where she doesn't know a soul. With the heart of a lion, she faces these fearful situations.

A female friend of mine put Kelsey's dilemma into perspective for me. We were eating lunch one day and she said, "I notice you have a cold sore on your lip. I bet you think everyone is looking at you, don't you?"

"I know they are," I replied.

"Well then you've gotten just a small taste of what your daughter faces every day."

Wow! That comment really punched me in the gut. I finally came close to understanding my daughter's situation. Worst of all, I know she was subjected to cruel teasing from other kids during her primary school years. For some reason I was clueless that this was taking place, and she never shared it with me. On the one hand, I regret not doing more to protect her; on the other hand, having to go through that adversity prepared her to face life's challenges and gave her compassion for those who are "different." As Kelsey says, "I feel God put me through a lot of teasing to help me with my own kids someday and of course to not be a stuck-up snob."

Every father wishes he could protect his kids from the vulgarity of life, but it seems like all of us have to go through a certain amount of pain, humiliation, and hurt in order to grow up. (Hey, at least I didn't name my son Sue!) All the tough incidents you endured, while they hurt, made you the person you are today. Life is tough. People who have been rescued too much do not fare very well. Courage is one of the character traits that allows a woman to boldly step forward in life to achieve her goals.

Sacrifice

Kelsey, while she is a very intelligent girl, never did well academically in school. The teaching style of most public education classrooms did not seem to connect with her learning style; she was bored and uninspired (and probably a little lazy as well). Thankfully she was a gifted athlete, playing both soccer and basketball in high school. These extracurricular activities are probably what kept her in school.

But by the summer between her junior and senior year, things finally came to a head. Kelsey was making poor choices in the friends she spent time with, she was barely passing all her classes, she had dropped all her sports, and she was pushing her boundaries at every possible chance. It was all we could do to keep her in school. I finally had enough. I gave her the option of switching to the high school my wife taught at or dropping out of school, getting her GED at the community college, and getting a full-time job. Her mother and I were both fed up with her nonsense.

What I did next shocked her. She claims I threw her in the car, drove out in the country, dropped her off in the middle of nowhere, and left her. That's not exactly what happened—but close! I did make her get in the car and drove her far into the country to a therapeutic horse ranch that worked with handicapped children and adults. I made her get out of the car, told the owner to put her to work, and left her there. I then drove her out there every day during the summer.

Kelsey started out "volunteering" by mucking the horse stalls. She slowly worked her way up until she was helping with the clients and horses. She eventually was hired as full-time staff and she continued to work there for the next couple of years. Miraculously, Kelsey's whole countenance soon dramatically changed. She became happier and more compliant, and she stopped hanging around with bad influences. When the school year started, she voluntarily switched high schools to where my wife worked. Suzanne connected her with several gifted teachers who developed programs to help her succeed. She even volunteered with the special needs PE classes. For the first time in her life, Kelsey made the honor roll! By taking the focus off her and placing it on those less fortunate than her, she matured and changed her entire attitude. In fact, to this day she continues to work with disadvantaged children and has a heart for those less fortunate than others.

A woman's life is composed of sacrifices. Being a good wife requires a great deal of sacrifice. Being a good parent requires a great deal of sacrifice. Having a career takes a lot of sacrifice. And I think being a good Christian requires a great deal of sacrifice. When we teach our daughters early in life the value of giving of ourselves to others in a noble cause, we allow them to learn the benefits of sacrifice. Marriage and parenting are both more about serving than they are about being served.

Boundaries and Discipline

The other day, Kelsey somewhat offhandedly said, "You're a lot nicer than you used to be." When I asked her what she meant, she said she didn't know exactly, but that I was just nicer now than when she was younger. Perhaps because she's an adult now our relationship has changed. Or maybe because I didn't come to Christ until she was about eight years old, she still remembers the "old" dad (my kids and wife have a before-Christ and after-Christ memory of Dad). But perhaps she is also remembering the fact that I set fairly stringent boundaries while she was growing up. These boundaries were used to teach her the self-discipline that she would need later on in life. I knew that as a strong-willed child she had a lot of traits that would serve her well in life. My challenge was to keep her from using those traits to self-destruct until she was mature enough to use them effectively.

Since she doesn't live under my roof now, my role is no longer that of disciplinarian or setter of boundaries. My role is now that of counselor, cheerleader, and even friend. Because of that I probably just seem nicer (or else I *was* a really mean father, which is a possibility). Nevertheless, our daughters need boundaries and discipline to teach them the consequences of the choices they make.

Part of protecting and training our daughters is to provide safe, healthy boundaries. Especially for strong-willed children, boundaries provide a safety net that keeps them from making harmful decisions until they are old enough to understand the consequences of their choices. Whether or not they are strong-willed, when girls become adolescents they typically start probing the strength and foundation of those boundaries. That is the time when they need boundaries the most. In fact, we noticed that our daughter tested those boundaries all through adolescence. When the boundaries were relaxed too much, she tended to start acting out and getting into trouble. When the boundaries were firmed up and back in place, she appeared to be more comfortable and relaxed. Those boundaries told her we loved her.

Don't be fooled, your teenage daughter is a master manipulator. She learns quickly how to get Daddy to do what she wants. She learns early that you don't like conflict, and she uses that to her advantage. One of the things I learned was to limit the amount of arguing I did with my daughter. Oftentimes teenage girls like to escalate arguments onto an emotional playing field. They do this intentionally. Resist this strategy—it's a trap! She has the advantage in any discussion that she can twist into an emotionally heated debacle. Arguing usually serves no purpose other than to give control to the child. Try and keep your disagreements as logical and simple as possible.

For instance, whenever Kelsey wanted to do something she knew we wouldn't let her do, she would start a discussion about it that would quickly escalate into an emotional shouting match. She would then feel vindicated in stomping off and slamming her door, all the while screaming "I hate you!" Later, in order to make amends and reconcile our relationship, we would usually capitulate to a lesser (although no less egregious) request on her part. Like a savvy flea market trader, the old negotiation strategy of demanding more than you really want, acting offended at the response, and finally settling for a compromise—which was what you really wanted in the first place—worked for her every time. However, if I could maintain my composure and only give logical reasons while resisting the urge to respond emotionally when she baited me, she would accept my decision without all the histrionics. She might not like my decision, but she had no ground to stand on against the truth of logic.

Sometimes the mere threat of the consequences of our actions is enough to keep our children in line. From about middle school on, any time Kelsey was giving me grief I just threatened to show up at her school in my tighty whities. She was horrified at the thought of her dad walking through her school in front of her friends with his hairy belly hanging out the bottom of his T-shirt and no pants on. She probably *thought* I wouldn't follow through on my threat, but she'd seen me do enough crazy stuff that she wasn't quite sure that I wouldn't either.

Young women desperately need boundaries. Most teenage girls have a compulsion to challenge the boundaries set for them. Oftentimes in a fit of anger or petulance, your daughter will threaten to do something you would not approve of. She might even threaten to do something that puts her in danger, gambling on your capitulating and giving in, or at least rescuing her. It is important in these circumstances to call her bluff. Otherwise girls have control of the relationship, and that is dangerous and frustrating for both dad and daughter.

Kelsey is two years younger than her brother, Frank. During the teenage years those two years are a big difference. Even though girls typically mature emotionally and even physically earlier than boys, the playing field is not always level. For instance, Frank, because he was older, often got to do things that we would not allow Kelsey to do, and he even had a later curfew in the evenings. Kelsey would take great umbrage at the fact that her brother got to do things she couldn't. Her mantra was, "How come Frank can and I can't?!" What Kelsey didn't realize was that the dangers out there are much greater for a beautiful seventeen-year-old blonde female than they are for a tree-trunk-sized, hairy nineteen-year-old young man. There are a whole lot more predators out there looking to rape and murder young girls than there are looking to sexually prey upon husky young males. And after midnight, most of the people roaming around are generally up to no good.

Your daughter does not need another friend—she has plenty of those. What she desperately needs is a father who has the courage and strength of character to hold her accountable to the boundaries in her life. She needs a father to parent her and guide her until she is capable of making healthy decisions on her own. While she is a teenager you should be allowing, even encouraging her to develop that decision-making process. But do not be fooled into thinking she is an adult and capable of concrete critical-thinking skills.

Suffering

Sometimes the greatest gift a father can give his daughter is to allow her to suffer. This is also the hardest thing for a father to do—I hate even saying it. But going through pain and suffering matures a person. It also toughens her and helps develop many character traits needed to succeed in life.

I have a longtime friend, client, and now advisor who raised two daughters successfully. I asked him if he had ever intentionally allowed one of his daughters to suffer in order to teach her a life lesson. The following, in his own words, is an instance when he was forced to allow one of his daughters to suffer, and the results.

Yes—but it was the hardest thing I ever had to do. Probably wouldn't have kept with it without my wife telling me it was for the best. I'm a real pushover for my daughters—they know it too. But the way it turned out was better than I imagined.

My daughter wanted to take a term off from college and work at a ski resort in Utah—not exactly hardship duty, or so it seemed at the time. The deal was that while she was in school, we were covering her costs. If she left school, she had to be on her own. We let her drive the car we gave her but insurance, gas, maintenance, housing, food, utilities—all other living expenses—were hers alone. She agreed.

She moved to Salt Lake, met a co-worker, and together they took a lease out on an apartment. She got a job as a barista at the resort and life was good . . . until her roommate decided she didn't want to pay rent anymore because she wasn't making enough money to pay rent *and* play. Her roommate split, leaving her with four months remaining on the lease and only a part-time job to cover it.

She was broke, hungry, alone but young—so she took a second job only to discover she still didn't make enough to pay her expenses. So she took a third job—worked about ten to twelve hours a day seven days a week, did no snowboarding at all (the cause for which she took the term off), got sick, and was still hungry, slightly less broke, and alone. I wanted so desperately to step in and bail her out—"just this one time"—but at the same time I realized that

171

she was learning a most valuable lesson of independence that she could not learn any other way. As I said, however, had it not been for my wife, I probably would have "helped the caterpillar out of the cocoon" and would have done more damage than good.

It was so difficult to be far away from her, knowing that just a little help would tide her over and feeling so bad that her roommate had stiffed her. But she found a resiliency and strength in God that I doubt she would have had I acted like God and bailed her out. I could have easily done so at the time, which made it even more difficult for me not to. But within a month or so, she had gotten over being sick, had settled down into a more sensible work routine, gotten a job at a restaurant where she made good tips, and finished out her lease term by herself. She still did very little snowboarding, but she did a lot of living independently—a lot of growing up, knowing that whatever life threw at her, she could survive and find both the strength and support needed in her relationship with God—and us.

She completed her obligations and told us she was ready to go back to school and finish this time—and she did, ultimately not only just getting her BA from Westminster but subsequently getting her master's from London School of Economics in health and community development. At one time I wondered if we were going to lose her to the snowboarding culture of irresponsibility and misdirection. To see where she's at today—happily married and living in London, working and deepening her love for God pretty much on her own as her husband has not yet assumed the reins of spiritual leadership—is all the more fulfilling.

Looking back, had I helped her in ways other than encouraging her, praying for her, and asking God to be her provider, this may not have turned out the same. Thank God for my wife.

I remember once listening to an elderly man who had raised many daughters give a presentation to a group of young fathers. The one thing he said that has stuck with me all these years was to make our daughters tough. He said, "Life is hard. Toughen your daughters so that life doesn't destroy them. Don't baby and pamper them so much that they cannot overcome the hardships of life."

This is a tough world, and in many ways it's tougher on women than it is on men.[1] Even within families it can be tougher on a girl than a boy. When a boy is raised with all sisters, he is generally spoiled. But when a girl is raised with all brothers, she is generally teased unmercifully.

Rescuing our daughters when they struggle prevents them from developing character. It also teaches them to quit during hardship. But life is hard, and those who learn to quit never succeed. They end up quitting on their marriage, their children, and themselves.

To teach those lessons you must hold your daughter accountable. When you set boundaries make sure you enforce them. If the rules keep changing or she knows she can change your mind by manipulation, it puts her in control and chaos results. Chaos does not produce security, consistency does.

Perseverance

The story of mountain man Hugh Glass is truly a remarkable testament to one man's grit, toughness, endurance, and perseverance. In 1823, while trapping with a group of other mountain men, Glass surprised a mother grizzly and her two cubs. The sow attacked Glass and badly mauled him before it was finally killed. Glass lost great quantities of blood and lapsed into a coma. Convinced he would die, the party leader asked for two volunteers to stay with him. Jim Bridger (then seventeen years old) and John Fitzgerald offered to stay and bury him. After a week, Glass was still barely alive when the party was reportedly attacked by Indians. Bridger and Fitzgerald fled with Glass's rifle, knife, and other equipment, incorrectly reporting he had died.

Glass later awoke from his coma to find himself abandoned, without weapons or equipment. He had suffered a broken leg, the cuts on his back were exposing bare ribs, and all his wounds were festering. He crawled to a nearby rotten log and rolled over on his back, allowing the maggots from the log to eat his dead, infected skin. Unable to walk, he set his own leg and then crawled through land occupied by hostile Indians and wild animals toward the nearest settlement, Fort Kiowa—over two hundred miles away. Surviving on berries, roots, and dead animals, it took him six weeks to reach the Cheyenne River. He then floated down the river, eventually reaching the fort. Glass recovered, and bent on revenge, he tracked down both Bridger and Fitzgerald. He forgave Bridger due to his young age and let Fitzgerald live because he was employed by the US Army.[2]

Wow! Talk about a man of grit and determination. That's the kind of man I want to be (minus the bear attack). Fathers who model that kind of perseverance teach their daughters the benefits of not giving up when things get difficult. I'm convinced we have created a culture that has made it easier for people, especially young people, to quit. As a culture we no longer have the stomach to suffer. There are no expectations to persevere through hardships. Most young people do not expect that their first marriage will last a lifetime. Hence we now have the phenomena of "starter marriages."

The problem with developing a habit of quitting is that the most important things in life are difficult to achieve. It is hard to succeed in our careers or to achieve our dreams and goals. Not only that, but the two most important relationships in life—marriage and children—are probably the most difficult. People who have learned to quit early in life tend to abandon their marriages and their children when things get difficult. They quit when they need to stay the most.

The Consequences of *Not* Teaching Her

Because I am a kinesthetic kind of individual, I enjoy physical activity—it's how I best learn new things and how I process information.

(I can always spot players on the basketball court who are kinesthetic—instead of diagramming a play on the blackboard, you have to physically walk them through it to develop "muscle memory" before they understand it.) Consequently I have enjoyed working out my whole life. In addition to the physical benefits, a strenuous workout releases endorphins that help regulate my mental and emotional health. I have had a gym membership most of my adult life, and even into my midfifties I enjoy working out with weights. Actually, I don't enjoy it so much anymore as I *have* to do it—otherwise I'd be fat as a hog. I try to do a power workout a couple of times a week along with some cardio workouts. As I've gotten older I've had to add some stretching and balancing programs as well. If I go too long without exercise, I get cranky and lethargic.

One thing I've discovered is that while working out at the gym may be hard, the alternative is worse. If you don't struggle and persevere through the pain, you never grow. But if you do struggle through the pain, you get the benefits of larger muscles, a more toned body, better conditioning, lowered stress, and a better self-image. Not to mention, staying in shape has other benefits as well. I once overheard one teenage boy tell another, "Kelsey's dad is buff—don't mess with her."

The same training principles may apply to raising a teenage girl. For the most part it will be difficult anyway. You might as well do it properly and struggle through the pain so you can get the benefits. If you do persevere through the hard times, you will gain the benefit of a well-rounded, healthy, loving daughter. The alternative is something that most fathers would rather not dwell upon.

FOR DISCUSSION AND REFLECTION

- If it's true that what we do speaks louder than what we say, what are some behaviors you need to change in your life so that you model good character for your daughter?

• What are some character traits you want to come to mind when someone mentions your daughter's name? How can you intentionally instill those traits into your daughter?

• Why is it important that a father allow his daughter to suffer? And why is it so hard to do?

11

The Father Blessing

An ounce of father is worth a ton of priest.

Old Spanish Proverb

Young people reflect the values of their family. The character of the relationship with their family of origin strongly affects their spiritual journey. Those values are the foundation they build their lives upon. Values contribute to the philosophy and worldview by which we live life. Young women who do not get a spiritual foundation early in life often struggle with the choices and decisions they make later on. Without a compass to steer them and guide their choices, they founder like a ship without a rudder.

The teen years are those years when a young woman's mind is expanding and the concepts of right and wrong, good and evil, and sacrifice and selfishness are finally starting to be understood. This is the time when she can start grasping complicated concepts such as religion and faith. This is the time when a father has his most significant impact on the spiritual development of his daughter.

Spiritual Development

Start developing your daughter's faith early in life. Kelsey was eight years old when I accepted Christ into my life. We immediately tried to live an authentic life of faith with our children, trying to make up for lost time as it were. Even though my daughter appeared to reject the Christian walk during her turbulent teenage years, she has come back and realizes the value of having God in her life. This is because of what was taught to her at a young age.

Another area to be aware of is how you present your faith to your daughter. The behaviors we model in faith always trump the words we use. As men and fathers our actions speak louder than our words. I remember when I closed the environmental engineering firm I had owned for sixteen years to go into full-time ministry, my then-teenage daughter approached me and tentatively asked, "Daddy, how are we going to live?"

Smiling, I said, "Well, I believe God will provide for us."

To which she frantically replied, "But what if he doesn't?"

"We'll worry about that when the time comes," I assured her.

Almost six years have passed since that day, and she has seen firsthand that the mortgage has been paid every month and that none of us ever missed a meal. I'm not sure how God has done that, but he has been faithful in providing our needs on a daily basis. My daughter has witnessed my faith in God and has grown in her faith because of it. She watched God miraculously provide for our needs even when it seemed hopeless. She has also watched God work through us to change the lives of others. And she has seen God bless us by showing us the fruits of our labor on a daily basis. Today, as a young woman her faith is strong and growing. She is seeking a relationship with God because she has seen one modeled in front of her eyes. She is also seeking a relationship with a young man who models that kind of faith as well.

Our model of faith is always more powerful than our words of faith. If you live a life of godly service in humility and faith, your daughter will internalize those values. If you live a hypocritical spiritual life where you look good on the outside but criticize and complain about others and never do anything to serve others outside the doors of the church, you will pass that attitude on to your daughter. If you have never risked anything for your faith, your daughter has probably never seen God answer your prayers.

Look for everyday examples or situations from your past where you can openly and honestly share your faith and how God has worked in your life. Don't be afraid to let your daughter know you made mistakes. Our kids know we are not perfect, so telling her where you have struggled in life and why God's presence was helpful is very important. Parents have a propensity to turn things into lectures. But sometimes less is more and actions always speak louder than words. Our example of living a godly life is a much more powerful message than any lecture could ever be.

Here's how one woman remembers her father:

> My dad has been a pastor (semi-retired now). One of my favorite memories was when he'd take me to church with him when my mom was busy. He'd work on his sermon and would allow me to take his mini-cassette recorder into the sanctuary. There I would preach, pray, lead in singing (making up the melody to the hymns) all on tape. If my "service" concluded before it was time to go home, I would then lead my invisible congregation in Sunday school. I think my dad was always my unconscious hero.

Prayer is also a powerful tool that fathers have at their disposal. Let your daughter see and hear you pray. Pray consistently for your daughter's spiritual, emotional, physical, and psychological health and safety. Pray God would bring healthy mentors and good friends into her life. Pray for her sexual purity. Pray for her future spouse and for his parents. Pray for wisdom and discernment. And pray for your daughter's decision making. My wife prayed daily that our children would get caught. She knew that they *would* make mistakes and poor choices. But if they got caught the first time they did something wrong, it would prevent them from harm or from continuing until the consequences were serious. I believe God answered those prayers, as our teens were continually baffled that they always got caught whenever they strayed from the path.

Many men find that being a spiritual leader in the home is difficult. But prayer is one way you can powerfully lead your family spiritually.

I once heard of a man who went into his daughter's room and prayed over her every night after she fell asleep. She grew up and left for college. The following Christmas she came home for a visit.

Talking to her mother one afternoon, she said, "Daddy still prays for me every night even though I'm away at college, doesn't he?"

"How in the world did you know that?" her mother replied.

The daughter replied with confidence, "I can still see his knee marks in the carpet next to my old bed."

Were you blessed to have a father who prayed faithfully for you when you were growing up? Only a small percentage of men answer yes when I ask that question. How do you think your life might have been different if you had a father who did that?

Try this experiment: go into your kids' rooms at night, kneel down, gently lay hands on their heads or backs, and petition God's blessings upon them. You'll find it a powerful moment. Your kids will stay very still under the blankets because, big or small, they recognize the significance of that act.

When your children know you are praying for them—praying for their sexual purity, for their salvation, for their future—this knowledge gives them a guidepost to hang onto. It also provides a form of accountability more powerful than bare parental authority.

When they see the knee marks next to their bed, it powerfully affects the kind of choices they make.

Even if your teenage daughter has walked away from her faith, do not lose hope. Many young people step away from the church and come back later. Your example of loving them instead of judging them is an important model of Christian faith. Loving them does not mean you are condoning their decisions or enabling them to continue destructive behaviors, but it does mean that you care enough to keep the relationship open. Your daughter's spiritual life is too important to close the doors on.

Why Dad Matters

Guys, we need to understand that a woman's father has a big influence in many areas of her life, but most especially in her view of her heavenly Father. A father's relationship with his daughter directly affects the relationship she has with God. The safety and security found in an earthly father's strong arms is your daughter's first concrete example of her heavenly Father's love and care. Understanding this will help you to meet some of the needs she has in her spiritual walk—and she needs your support, strength, and leadership in this area!

A common theme among women who did not have a father is the inability to trust a man and believe that she won't be abandoned again. Depending on and loving a man is a leap of faith, because for these women a permanent relationship with a man is theoretical.[1] And so women who suffer from father wounds also tend to struggle with developing a close relationship with God as well. They cannot believe that he will not abandon them like their earthly father did. To admit that their earthly father loved them so little that he left them is difficult enough. Imagine how devastating it would be to think that the Creator of the universe wouldn't love them enough to stay.

Without a father around to provide a role model, healthy physical affection, and protection for her, a girl is left to the examples of masculinity she sees on television, in the movies, and in music videos—by all accounts very poor options. She then transfers these images onto God. If her father and other older males in her life abandoned her, ignored her, or abused her, how can she possibly trust a heavenly Father? How can she risk fully giving her heart to someone who might once again leave?

A father models for his daughter the qualities she looks for in men, the standards she maintains, and ultimately the qualities she attributes to God. He is the first man in her life and models how a man should treat a woman, how a man should act, and how a man shows healthy love and affection to a woman. He also sets the standard for how a daughter feels she deserves to be treated by men. He even determines how a girl feels about herself. He determines how a girl believes God should view her and treat her.

If a father shows his daughter love, respect, and appreciation for who she is, she will believe that about herself as a woman, no matter what anyone else thinks. How her father felt about her is how she will project God feels about her. I know one wonderful, competent woman who believes that God does not trust her. She is a successful single mom who owns her own home and has a good job and great kids. Why would she believe she is incompetent and untrustworthy? Because she had a father who always criticized her and told her she was worthless. Even though intellectually she knows that she isn't worthless, her heart will not allow her to believe any different.

I cannot tell you how many men contact me who are struggling in their relationship with their wives. Many of them report that their wife will not trust them, will not open up and be intimate, or will not give them the respect they crave, no matter what they do to encourage and nurture her. After looking closely into each woman's background, we discover that most of these women had been severely wounded by their earthly fathers.

Despite the guard that so many women put up (claiming the lack of a father does not matter), it is clear that not having a father affects them greatly. How could it not? It also affects their perspective of God. After all, if a woman cannot entrust her heart to an earthly father, how can she entrust it to a heavenly Father? That causes her to trust her husband less and to be more guarded and less intimate. A woman like this is less likely to allow herself to be vulnerable and to allow a man to serve and lead her.

God's Daughter

We all know people who believe themselves to be stupid or incompetent. They get this perspective from their experiences in life, the way their caretakers treated them as children, society's mores, cultural bias and messages, and spiritual attacks upon them. But the lens we see ourselves through rarely shows reality. For instance, many girls and women believe in their hearts that they are physically unattractive, overweight, or have any number of other negative characteristics. In their minds this makes them less loveable, less worthy, less valuable as a person. The mirror they see themselves in is cracked or warped and reflects a distorted view or perception of them back to their eyes. In their hearts they mourn their perceived lack of lovability and worth. They do not see themselves as God sees them—as beautiful daughters of Eve.

As a father you have the ability to filter the lens that your daughter sees herself through. Women and girls tend to look at their flaws through a magnifying glass instead of looking at themselves as a whole. My wife likes to hike in the mountains near where we live. She often comes across gorgeous settings that take her breath away. But if she were to look at the pieces of the scene individually, she would notice that the ground is covered with animal scat, the pine needles are sticky with sap, the trees are covered with bugs, and the flowers are dirty and have bees around them. Individually the scene is not so beautiful, but taken as a whole it is a magnificent example of God's beautiful creation. The same is true with women. If they only look at their flaws and not at the whole picture, they will never be satisfied and will never see God's magnificent creation.

This self-misperception makes women susceptible to the affections (physical or verbal) of earthly men who would use them for their own self-gratification. It also prevents them from receiving the love and grace of a heavenly Father who wants them to know how glorious and spectacular he created them to be. Author Steven James says, "Inside of every woman lives a needy little girl wanting to feel pretty, loved, secure. Expose her to her imperfections, toy with her desire to feel loved, rattle her sense of security, and you bring that needy little girl to the surface."[2]

We all have wounds in our hearts or holes in our souls. Many people try to fill those empty spaces with drugs, alcohol, sex, power, or money to deaden the pain. But the truth is only God's love and forgiveness can fill those wounds. Those wounds and the ways we try to soothe them also contribute to this distortion of how God perceives us. Many women believe that because of things they've done or mistakes they've made in the past, God will not or cannot forgive them. This is just not true, but guilt prevents them from allowing God's forgiveness to enter their hearts. God can heal those wounds, but we must open them up and give them to him so that through his forgiveness, love, grace, and mercy, we can eventually forgive ourselves and even learn to love ourselves. Once we love ourselves we can love others with even more grace, depth, and beauty.

One of the ways we fathers can develop self-worth in our daughters is by how we treat their mothers. Husbands—with the power God has given us as one of the two most powerful men in a woman's life along with her father—we have the ability to counteract our wives' self-criticisms by giving them honest verbal affirmations, by treating them with honor, dignity, and respect, and by loving them unconditionally.

Here is how one woman described her husband and her search for fatherly love: "This was the first man ever who treated me with respect and dignity. Who loved me for who I was and not for what I could give him. And for the first time, I felt like I deserved it and was worthy of it. My biological father should have taught me that a long time ago. But he didn't. I learned it from my heavenly Father."

Guys, you are the only other man in the world who can counteract any negative self-perceptions your wife's father or the world might have placed upon her. As her husband you are the only other man God has granted the power to influence her at the core of her being. As men we know we have fragile egos regarding our performance and our adequacy. Your wife's self-image regarding her beauty and value as a woman is just as fragile. When you love her, cherish her, respect her, and honor her, it can heal some of those wounds that damaged her heart. Please be conscious of that power and use it responsibly. If you use it poorly or not at all, it can cause even greater, irreversible damage.

Teach your daughter that God loves her just the way he created her. She is a daughter of Eve, the magnificent culmination of his creation. It doesn't matter what she looks like, how much she weighs, how smart and accomplished she is, or how many mistakes she's made. God loves the inside of her—her heart—her entire being. That part deep down inside her that she never shares with anyone else. He knows her even better than she knows herself—all of her imperfections and faults. Yet he still loves her unconditionally and willingly forgives all of her sins and shortcomings. He always welcomes his children home with a father's loving arms, no matter how far they've strayed.

Earthly Father/Heavenly Father

Most people agree that the perception a woman has regarding her heavenly Father is in direct proportion to the perception she has of her earthly father. Her earthly father determines how a girl believes God should view her and treat her.

One day as my wife and I were driving, we listened to a radio program. The guest was Angela Thomas, the author of books such as *Do You Think I'm Beautiful?* and *My Single Mom Life.* Angela was describing her struggles as a single mom being exhausted and overwhelmed by all the pressures of having four small children. She spoke about crying out to God and telling him she couldn't handle any more. God responded, she said, by paternally loving her, encouraging her, and calling her his "sweet baby girl."

I looked over at my wife, noticed she was crying, and asked her what was wrong. She said, "Never having had a father, I can't even imagine a loving heavenly Father calling me his sweet baby girl."

Angela is from the South, and my being a little thickheaded I responded, "Well, maybe that's a Southern thing."

Almost sobbing now, my wife said, "No, you call Kelsey your sweet baby girl all the time. It must be a dad thing!"

Later as she was relating that story to our daughter, even before she could get to the part about me calling her my sweet baby girl, Kelsey blurted out, "Daddy calls me his sweet baby girl!"

She then went on to tell my wife about a little note I gave her years ago. I don't even remember what it said—something about how you can only truly live when you take the focus off yourself and put it on others. But Kelsey apparently reads it every day and has it memorized. She keeps it on the bathroom counter in her apartment to look at every morning. But the most important part of the note was that it was signed, "I love you Sweet Baby Girl, love Daddy."

It humbles me to think that those few simple words from her father mean so much to her. Even more humbling is that her image of her heavenly Father makes a relationship with him more easily accessible due in some small part to the example I set as her earthly father.

The Power of Your Voice

A father's voice has special power in a child's life. His deep voice is comforting to his daughter. Teachers often report that father figures who volunteer at schools tend to have a calming effect on the classroom. Men usually don't have to raise their voice to get the attention of their daughters. One woman who had been widowed for a long time told me that when it was just her and the girls in the home, things tended to get loud and chaotic. After a period of many years she finally remarried and was pleasantly surprised to learn how having a man's deep voice in the home had a calming effect on everyone. She said, "We didn't realize just how much we missed a man's presence and how comforting it made us feel just to hear his voice." My wife has told me that when I am traveling the thing she misses most is my voice. She feels safer, more secure, and sleeps better when she hears me at home.

God has given men power through their voices to garner the attention of females who love them. Proverbs talks about a wise man's words being "a honeycomb, sweet to the soul and healing to the bones" (Prov. 16:24). That means they taste good and are healing to those who hear them. Ecclesiastes 12:11 likens a wise man's words to goads—they give heart and courage to the person spoken to.

Most men do not enjoy talking all that much, and many are men of few

Things a Daughter Needs to Hear from Her Dad

- You are beautiful just the way you are.
- You look just like a young woman is supposed to look.
- You look just like God designed women to look.
- God created you special and unique.
- You are brilliant and intelligent.
- I love what a good person you are on the inside.
- I love you and I'm so proud of you.
- You can never do anything that will stop me from loving you.
- I will always be your dad—I will always be here for you.
- God has a plan for your life.
- God loves you unconditionally.

words. In fact, if you are like me, you despise people who babble on without ever getting to the point. But if we never use this power, if we never talk to our daughters, we waste the gift that God has given us.

Blessing Her

This past year Kelsey (then twenty-one years old) and I were blessed to be asked to speak at a father-daughter conference in Seattle. It was a powerful event that was attended by about sixty pairs of fathers and their daughters whose ages ranged from eleven to twenty-five years old. The conference was an all-day event sponsored by several fathering and family ministries. The program consisted of seven sessions working with fathers and daughters together, fathers alone, and daughters alone by age group. Each session was designed to build upon the previous ones and included inspirational speakers, letter writing, trust-building exercises, and father-daughter dialogues. The goal of the weekend was to help the fathers understand how important they are in the lives of their daughters, and how to foster a healthy connection with their daughters as they become young women. We also wanted to help the daughters recognize their need for a healthy relationship with their fathers and the consequences in their lives when that doesn't happen. Finally, we wanted to help facilitate reconciliation between fathers and daughters who were struggling or had past wounds.

As the teenage girls arrived, their body language strongly suggested that they did not want to be there, and many of them were actually cold and distant toward their fathers. The dads, of course, appeared a bit anxious and nervous. But as the day progressed and the speakers and workshops broke down those barriers, we began to see fathers and daughters talking, sitting closer to one another, and even laughing and hugging each other.

The event culminated in a "father blessing" of the daughters. I knelt in front of my daughter onstage and prayerfully offered my blessing to her publicly, stating that I loved her, I was proud of her, and asking God to bestow his blessings upon her. (Yes, it was difficult to keep from blubbering.) I don't remember all that I said, but I do remember Kelsey then tearfully accepted my blessing and responded with gratitude and thankfulness for me being her father (stupid eyes wouldn't stop watering). To then watch as each father knelt and blessed his daughter was a powerful and emotional experience. It was too much for one previously sullen young girl who threw her arms around her father, buried her face in his chest, and sobbed, "Oh Daddy, I love you so much!" Many fathers and daughters were in tearful embraces as we concluded the day's activities.

Even though my daughter and I had a close relationship before this event, I truly believe that my publicly proclaiming a blessing over her changed and deepened our relationship. She appears much calmer around me now—more confident in my love for her. Even though I told her all those years that I loved her, my willingness to risk humiliation to prove it must have somehow cemented it in her soul. It is similar to the public declaration we make to Christ when we are baptized.

You don't need to attend a father-daughter event to bless your daughter. You can do it every day by speaking a blessing over her. When you speak into her heart all the things you love and cherish about her, you fill her soul with nourishment she will live on for the rest of her life.

Your father blessings can make the difference between a life of joy and contentment or one of anguish and despair. God has given fathers the ability through their words and actions to bless the lives of their children. As with all great power comes great responsibility. Use your power wisely and you in turn will be blessed by generations of your lineage being healthy, happy children of God.

In closing, just love your daughter. Love covers a multitude of sins. You never know when circumstances may take ones you love. My sister was killed by a drunk driver when she was seventeen years old. It was a horribly grieving experience. I cannot imagine how much more it would hurt to lose a daughter. So just love your daughter like she might not be there tomorrow. Love her like you might never see her again—because that could very easily happen. If you don't love her that way and something does happen, you'll regret it for the rest of your life. You do *not* want to carry those kinds of regrets around with you. You can see the haunted look in the eyes of men who have either lost a daughter to death or lost her to a rift in their relationship.

If you have lost contact or are estranged from your daughter, I want you to know it is never too late. If you have unresolved issues with your daughter, I encourage you to have the courage to approach her to reconcile them. If your relationship is not at the level you would like it to be, I hope you will strive to make amends. Your daughter needs you in her life and you need her in your life. Take the steps necessary to resolve your differences. Too often our pride or fear of rejection keeps one or both parties from reaching out to the other. Swallow your pride and reach out to her in repentance. Ask for her forgiveness if necessary. Be a man, take the first step, and continue to seek her out, regardless of how hopeless it may seem.

God bless you and your daughter.

FOR DISCUSSION AND REFLECTION

• In what ways does an earthly father represent the heavenly Father in his daughter's life?

- Have you decided on a strategy to intentionally bless your daughter by giving her a "father's blessing"? This is too important to put off, guys. By yourself—or better, with some other fathers with daughters—develop a plan to look for and create opportunities to bless your daughter. She needs this throughout her life, not just as a onetime event.

Notes

Chapter 1 What Are Little Girls Made Of?

1. "Fetal Development: First Trimester," American Pregnancy Association, accessed September 9, 2010, http://www.americanpregnancy.org/duringpregnancy/fetaldevelopment1.htm.

2. J. Bland, *About Gender: Conception and Development* (1998), http://www.gender.org.uk/about/04embryo/44_cncp.htm.

3. Joanna Infeld, "The Differences between Boys and Girls," Suite101.com, accessed April 28, 2010, http://www.suite101.com/content/the-differences-between-boys-and-girls-a226314.

4. Ibid.

5. "Girls and Puberty," 4Parents.gov, accessed June 3, 2010, http://www.4parents.gov/sexdevt/girlswomen/index.html.

6. Michael Gurian, *The Wonder of Girls* (New York: Atria Books, 2002), 71–73.

7. Ibid., 79.

8. Ibid., 79–80.

9. Ibid., 80.

10. Michael Gurian, *A Fine Young Man* (New York: Putnam, 1998), 38–40.

11. Gurian, *The Wonder of Girls*, 33.

12. "Brain Imaging Shows How Men and Women Cope Differently under Stress," adapted from materials provided by University of Pennsylvania School of Medicine, ScienceDaily, November 20, 2007, http://www.sciencedaily.com/releases/2007/11/071119170133.htm.

13. Gurian, *The Wonder of Girls*, 34.

14. Ibid., 38.

15. Ibid., 39.

16. "All About Menstruation," TeensHealth, accessed July 30, 2010, http://kidshealth.org/teen/sexual_health/girls/menstruation.html#.

17. The National Women's Health Information Center, US Dept. of Health and Human Services, womenshealth.gov, http://www.womenshealth.gov/faq/menstruation.cfm.

18. "Menstrual Cycles: What Really Happens in Those 28 Days?" Women's Health Information, Feminist Women's Health Center, http://www.fwhc.org/health/moon.htm.

19. From chapter 10, "Images of PMS," in Daniel Amen, *Images of Human Behavior: A Brain Spect Atlas* (Newport Beach, CA: Mindworks, 2004), 10–11.

20. Ibid.

21. Ibid.

Chapter 2 Her Father's Influence

1. Meg Meeker, *Strong Fathers, Strong Daughters* (Washington, DC: Regnery, 2006), 8.

2. Ibid., 23, citing M. Esterbrook and Wendy A. Goldberg, "Toddler Development in the Family: Impact of Father Involvement and Parenting Characteristics," *Child Development* 55 (1984): 740–52.

3. Meeker, *Strong Fathers, Strong Daughters*, 23, citing Coley, "Children's Socialization Experiences and Functioning in Single-Mother Households."

4. Meeker, *Strong Fathers, Strong Daughters*, 23, citing *Journal of the American Medical Association* 10 (September 10, 1997): 823–32; and Greg J. Duncan, Martha Hill, and W. Jean Yeung, "Fathers' Activities and Childrens' Attainments," paper presented at a conference on father involvement, October 10–11, Washington, DC, found in: Wade F. Horn and Tom Sylvester, *Father Facts 4*, www.fatherhood.org.

5. Meeker, *Strong Fathers, Strong Daughters*, 24.

6. Lois Mowday, *Daughters without Dads: Offering Understanding and Hope to Women Who Suffer from the Absence of a Loving Father* (Nashville: Oliver-Nelson Books, 1990), 64.

7. Ibid.

8. Ibid.

9. Dr. Kevin Leman, *What a Difference a Daddy Makes* (Nashville: Thomas Nelson, 2000), 6.

10. Ibid., 62.

11. Gleaned from Rick Johnson, "Is There a Difference in Educational Outcomes in Students from Single Parent Homes?" (master's thesis, Concordia University, 2009).

12. Victoria Secunda, *Women and Their Fathers: The Sexual and Romantic Impact of the First Man in Your Life* (New York: Delacorte, 1992), 211.

13. Angela Thomas, *Do You Think I'm Beautiful? The Question Every Woman Asks* (Nashville: Thomas Nelson, 2003), 52.

14. Ken Canfield, *The Heart of a Father* (Chicago: Northfield, 1996), 19–20.

15. Bill Bright, "Committed to Marriage," in *A Life of Integrity*, ed. Howard Hendricks (Sisters, OR: Multnomah, 1997), 79–80.

16. Leman, *What a Difference*, 85.

Chapter 3 Communicating with the Female Species

1. Leman, *What a Difference,* 107.
2. Chap Clark and Dee Clark, *Daughters and Dads: Building a Lasting Relationship* (Colorado Springs: Navpress, 1998), 29.
3. Michael Gurian, *The Wonder of Boys* (New York: Putnam, 1996), adapted from pp. 14–15.

Chapter 4 Bonding with Girls

1. Meeker, *Strong Fathers, Strong Daughters*, 96.
2. Clark and Clark, *Daughters and Dads*, 54
3. "Rock of Gibraltar," Wikipedia, accessed June 9, 2010, http://en.wikipedia.org/wiki/Rock_of_Gibraltar.

Chapter 5 What a Girl Needs from Her Father

1. Joe Kemp, Jill Colvin, and Rich Schapiro, "California Dad Makes Heroic Rescue of Daughter, 2, After She Falls 20 Feet Off Ramp into East River," *New York Daily News*, April 3, 2010, http://www.nydailynews.com/ny_local/2010/04/03/2010-04-03_east_river_rescue_tourist_saves_2yrold_daughter_who_fell_off_peking_ship_at_sout.html.
2. Meeker, *Strong Fathers, Strong Daughters*, 30.
3. Joe Kelly, "Tips for Dads of Daughters," Fatherville.com monthly newsletter, April 5, 2005, www.fatherville.com.
4. Diane Ravitch, *The Language Police: How Pressure Groups Restrict What Students Learn* (New York: Vintage, 2004).
5. "Politically Correct," s.v. "The Language Police," Conservapedia, accessed August 6, 2010, http://www.conservapedia.com/Politically_correct.
6. George Orwell, *1984*, part 1, chapter 3, http://www.george-orwell.org/1984/2.html.
7. David Kupelian, *How Evil Works* (New York: Simon & Schuster, 2010), 14.
8. Quoted in Ibid., 14–15.

Chapter 6 "Danger, Will Robinson!"

1. Gurian, *The Wonder of Girls*, 44.
2. Leman, *What a Difference*, 119.
3. Kelly, "Tips for Dads of Daughters."
4. Vicki Courtney, *Five Conversations You Must Have with Your Daughter* (Nashville: Broadman & Holman, 2008), 26.
5. Joan Jacobs Brumberg, *The Body Project: An Intimate History of American Girls* (1998), xxiv, cited in Courtney, *Five Conversations*, 18.
6. Thomas Perry, *Pursuit* (New York: Random House, 2001), 214.
7. "Factors That May Contribute to Eating Disorders," National Eating Disorders Association, accessed August 12, 2010, http://www.nationaleatingdisorders.org/uploads/file/information-resources/Factors%20that%20may%20Contribute%20to%20Eating%20Disorders.pdf.

8. Joan Jacobs Brumberg, *Fasting Girls: the Emergence of Anorexia Nervosa as a Modern Disease* (Cambridge: Harvard University Press, 1988), quoted in Courtney, *Five Conversations*, 24.

9. "Learn Basic Terms and Information on a Variety of Eating Disorder Topics," National Eating Disorders Association, accessed August 12, 2010, http://www.nationaleatingdisorders.org/information-resources/general-information.php#terms-definitions.

10. Ibid.

11. Quoted in Courtney, *Five Conversations*, 20.

12. Davi Nabors, "Broadening the Image of Beauty," *Vancouver Family Magazine*, August 2010, 12–14.

13. "Eating Disorder," Wikipedia, accessed August 12, 2010, http://en.wikipedia.org/wiki/Eating_disorder.

14. Michael Robotham, *Suspect* (New York: Doubleday, 2005), 58.

15. Dr. Wendy Lader, quoted in Jeanie Lerche Davis, "Cutting and Self-Harm: Warning Signs and Treatment," WebMD, accessed August 15, 2010, http://www.webmd.com/mental-health/features/cutting-self-harm-signs-treatment.

16. Ibid., quoting David Rosen, MD, MPH, who is professor of pediatrics at the University of Michigan and director of the Section for Teenage and Young Adult Health at the University of Michigan Health Systems in Ann Arbor.

17. Ibid.

18. "New Terrible Teen Fad—Self-Embedding," HealthDay News, *Oregon Women's Report*, accessed September 9, 2010, http://oregonwomensreport.com/2010/09/new-terrible-teen-fad-self-embedding/.

19. Meeker, *Strong Fathers, Strong Daughters*, 21.

20. Ibid., 87.

21. Courtney, *Five Conversations*, 126, citing Wendy Shalit, *Girls Gone Mild*, the National Longitudinal Survey of Adolescent Health, Wave II (1996).

22. Courtney, *Five Conversations*, 126, citing Robert E. Rector, Kirk A. Johnson, and Lauren R. Noyes, "Sexually Active Teenagers Are More Likely to Be Depressed and Attempt Suicide," Heritage Center for Data Analysis, 2003, www.heritage.org.

23. David Kupelian, *How Evil Works* (New York: Simon & Schuster, 2010), 80, citing Jean M. Twinge and W. Keith Campbell, *The Narcissism Epidemic: Living in the Age of Entitlement* (New York: Simon & Schuster, 2009), introduction.

24. Gurian, *The Wonder of Girls*, 250.

Chapter 7 Protecting Her

1. Meeker, *Strong Fathers, Strong Daughters*, 18.

2. Mike Trihey, "Reporter: Weaver's Dad Was Pure Evil," *Portland Tribune*, September 3, 2002, http://www.portlandtribune.com/news/story.php?story_id=13543.

3. John Darling, "Stand Up for Yourself and Others: Local Author Teaches Children about Being Confident, and Says if They See Bullying Happen, Try to Stop It," *The Mail Tribune*, January 30, 2009, http://www.mailtribune.com/apps/pbcs.dll/article?AID=/20090130/NEWS/901300328&cid=sitesearch.

4. Deedra Hunter and Elizabeth Whittemore, "Very Mean Girls—Two Generations Look at Abusive Females," March 12, 2009, The Lifeworks Group, Inc., http://lifeworksgroup.blogspot.com/2009/03/very-mean-girls-2-generations-look-at.html.

5. Paul Coughlin, "Bullying Defined," Crosswalk.com, November 11, 2008, http://www.crosswalk.com/parenting/11595601/.

6. Quoted in Courtney, *Five Conversations*, 97–98.

7. "Pater Familias," Wikipedia, accessed June 1, 2010, http://en.wikipedia.org/wiki/Patria_potestas.

8. "Marriage in Ancient Rome," Wikipedia, accessed June 1, 2010, http://en.wikipedia.org/wiki/Marriage_in_ancient_Rome.

9. "Statistics Surrounding Child Sexual Abuse," Darkness to Light, accessed June 7, 2010, http://www.darkness2light.org/knowabout/statistics_2.asp.

10. "Reporting Rates," RAINN: Rape, Abuse & Incest National Network citing the 2005 Department of Justice National Crime Victimization Study, accessed June 7, 2010, http://www.rainn.org/get-information/statistics/reporting-rates.

11. Rita A. Stratton, "The Long-Term Effects of Sexual Abuse on Girls," *The Mt. Hood–Gorge Connection*, November 26, 2009, 9.

12. Ibid.

Chapter 8 The Truth about Boys

1. "Boys Growing Up," BBC Science & Nature, January 8, 2010, http://www.bbc.co.uk/science/humanbody/body/articles/lifecycle/teenagers/boy_s_growth.shtml.

2. Meeker, *Strong Fathers, Strong Daughters*, 3.

Chapter 9 Uh-Oh! She's Becoming a Woman!

1. Meeker, *Strong Fathers, Strong Daughters*, 98.

2. Gurian, *The Wonder of Girls*, 269.

3. *The Oregonian*, "Study Finds Girls Developing Earlier," *New York Times* News Service, August 9, 2010, 2. Also see Kathleen Doheny, "Study: Girls Entering Puberty Earlier: By Age 7, Breast Development More Common Than Reported 10 to 30 Years Ago," WebMD Children's Health, accessed August 9, 2010, http://children.webmd.com/news/20100809/study-girls-entering-puberty-earlier.

4. Society for the Advancement of Education, "Father-Daughter Relationship Is Crucial—Effect on Age When Puberty Begins—Brief Article," *USA Today*, December 1999, http://findarticles.com/p/articles/mi_m1272/is_2655_128/ai_58037917/?tag=rbxcra.2.a.33.

5. Excerpted from an article by Candis McLean, "Daddy's Girl Matures Later—Stepfathers Are Shown to Produce 'Precocious Puberty' in Young Females," *Report Newsmagazine*, April 16, 2001, 46.

6. Kaiser Family Foundation, "U.S. Teen Sexual Activity," January 2005, citing a 2003 CDC Youth Risk Behavior Survey, http://www.kff.org/youthhivstds/upload/U-S-Teen-Sexual-Activity-Fact-Sheet.pdf.

7. Ibid., citing a 2002 study by the Alan Guttmacher Institute, http://www.kff.org/youthhivstds/upload/U-S-Teen-Sexual-Activity-Fact-Sheet.pdf.

8. Meeker, *Strong Fathers, Strong Daughters*, 24.

9. Ibid.

10. "How Is the 34% Statistic Calculated?" National Campaign to Prevent Teen Pregnancy fact sheet, Washington, DC: NCPTP, 2004.

11. R. A. Maynard, *Kids Having Kids: A Robin Hood Foundation Special Report on the Costs of Adolescent Childbearing* (New York: Robin Hood Foundation, 1996).

12. American Social Health Association/Kaiser Family Foundation, "STDs in America: How Many Cases and at What Cost?" 1998, http://www.kff.org/youth hivstds/upload/U-S-Teen-Sexual-Activity-Fact-Sheet.pdf.

Chapter 10 Character Training

1. Leman, *What a Difference*, 89.

2. "Hugh Glass," Wikipedia, accessed May 25, 2010, http://en.wikipedia.org/wiki/Hugh_Glass.

Chapter 11 The Father Blessing

1. Secunda, *Women and Their Fathers*, 211.

2. Steven James, *The Rook* (Grand Rapids: Revell, 2008), 366–67.

Bestselling author and speaker **Rick Johnson** founded Better Dads, a fathering skills program based on the urgent need to empower men to lead and serve in their families and communities. Rick's books have expanded his ministry to include influencing the whole family, with life-changing insights for men and women on parenting, marriage, and personal growth. He is a sought-after speaker at many large conferences across the United States and Canada and is a popular keynote speaker at men's and women's retreats and conferences on parenting and marriage. Rick is also a nationally recognized expert in several areas, including the effects of fatherlessness, and has been asked to teach at various educational venues.

To find out more about Rick Johnson, his books, and the Better Dads ministry, or to schedule workshops, seminars, or speaking engagements, please visit www.betterdads.net.

Meet

RICK JOHNSON

at www.BetterDads.net

Connect with Rick on Facebook

f *Rick Johnson*

t *@betterdads4u*

ENCOURAGEMENT FOR FATHERS IN THEIR MOST IMPORTANT ROLE

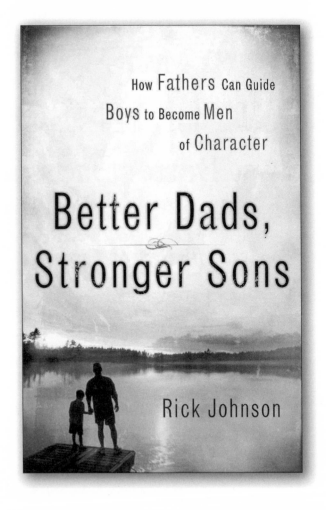

How Fathers Can Guide Boys to Become Men of Character

Better Dads, Stronger Sons

Rick Johnson

R Revell
a division of Baker Publishing Group
www.RevellBooks.com

Available Wherever Books Are Sold
Also Available in Ebook Format

HOW DOES A BOY BECOME A MAN OF CHARACTER?

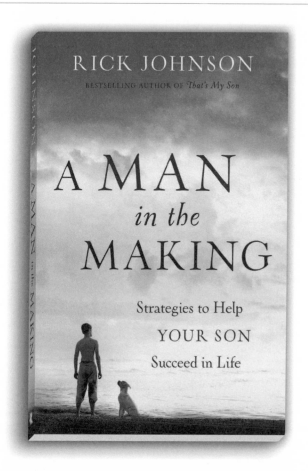

Highlighting famous men throughout history and the character trait that made each an outstanding model of manhood, parenting expert Rick Johnson gives you strategies to help mold your son into an honorable man.

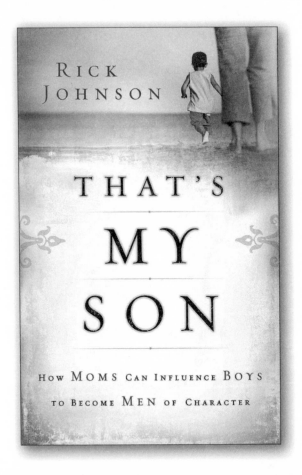